A-Z Guide to Children and Young People's Digital Mental Health

An Essential Resource for Parents, Educators and Professionals

Becca Randell

A to Z Guide to Children and Young People's Digital Mental Health

An essential resource for parents, educators and professionals

Published by:
Pavilion Publishing and Media Ltd
Blue Sky Offices, 25 Cecil Pashley Way, Shoreham by Sea,
West Sussex, BN43 5FF

Tel: +44 (0)1273 434943
Email: info@pavpub.com
Web: www.pavpub.com

Published 2025

A catalogue record for this book is available from the British Library.

ISBN: 978-1-803884-07-3

Pavilion Publishing and Media is a leading publisher of books, training materials and digital content in mental health, social care and allied fields. Pavilion and its imprints offer must-have knowledge and innovative learning solutions underpinned by sound research and professional values.

Author: Becca Randell
Copy editor: Jo Hathaway
Cover design: Phil Morash, Pavilion Publishing and Media Ltd
Page layout and typesetting: Emma Dawe, Pavilion Publishing and Media Ltd
Printing: Independent Publishers Group (IPG)

To Paul, Ethan and Iris - thank you for your support, love and belief in both me and this book. This is for you and all those parents, teachers and professionals as you navigate your own and your children's digital journeys.

Acknowledgements

I would like to thank all the hundreds of parents, carers and professionals that generously gave up their time to meet with me individually or collectively and complete a survey to share their views of children and young people's digital mental health. I would also like to thank the children and young people who so kindly and honestly shared their online experiences and allowed me to document their insight within this guide to help develop the resources and activities.

I would especially like to thank Paul, my wonderful husband who provided endless tech support and patiently supported me whilst I drafted this in between work and whilst travelling across South America – from Brazil to Bolivia. Thank you to my gorgeous young adults - Iris and Ethan who helped by sharing their online experiences and giving me encouragement whilst writing this Guide.

My thanks also go to Louisa Robertson, Jo Hathaway, Caitlin Gleeson and the team at Pavillion Publishing who were brilliantly supportive by allowing me to create this resource on a subject I feel so passionately about.

A special thanks to Dr Devyn Glass, Millie Robinson and Amanda Ferrell, from University of Sussex for helping design and analyse the survey for parents, carers and professionals.

A thanks goes to some of the key young experts who have helped share their insight on gaming, influencers and social media – Abi Sansome, Owen and Aidan Randell, Bel Gould, Lauren Ukrainec, Theo Williams and many more who asked to remain anonymous.

On this journey I have met some fantastic people who through their expertise have offered their professional experiences and knowledge which has fed into this guide. This includes, Alexandra Evans from 5Rights Foundation, Caroline Adams QPM, Digital Youth Engagement, Police, Cliff Manning from Parentzone, James Houghton from Future Voices, Bex Pink and Jay Jones from National Youth Agency, Dr Faith Orchard from University of East Anglia, Jo Hillier from Sussex Partnership Foundation NHS Trust, Dr Bryan Singer from University of Sussex, Lisa Debrou from Credo Therapies, Professor Robin Banerjee from University of Sussex, Kate Taylor and Rani Govender from NSPCC, Dr Emily Setty from University of Surrey, Paul Phillips and the Essex Digivators from Essex County Council and Amit Kalley from For Working Parents.

About the Author

Becca Randell is a Children's Digital Consultant and the Founder of Empowering Digital Lives which aims to help parents and professionals including teachers to support not only themselves but also children and young people to thrive online through digital literacy as well as safety and digital mental wellbeing (www.empoweringdigitallives.com).

She is currently leading the mobilisation of digital mental health innovation as part of the Health Innovation Network and the implementation of research in children and young people's mental health for National Institute of Health and Care (NIHR) Applied Research Collaboration. With over 25 years' experience of strategic commissioning and operational management of maternity, mental health and children and young people's services, her passion lies with improving outcomes for children and their families especially those who are the most under-represented.

As Honorary Research Fellow at University of Sussex, Becca has extensive experience of leading research and developing evidence-based interventions in mental health. Whilst supporting innovators and clinicians in developing, marketing and implementing digital mental health innovation she has also undertaken research and co-produced toolkits and resources for schools, innovators, commissioners, children and young people which she has presented internationally and nationally.

In her spare time, Becca is Vice President and founding trustee of Dementia Support and trustee for Stonepillow, a local charity supporting homeless people. She is a mum of two wonderful young "adults" and has drafted this book to help other parents and professionals recognise the impact of technology on not only their own mental wellbeing but also the wellbeing of their children and young people.

Contents

Full colour resources are available online at

www.pavpub.com/mental-health/a-to-z-guide-to-children-and-young-peoples-digital-mental-health-resources

from where they can be downloaded and printed.

Prologue

As a mum of two "young adults" and a career of working in mental health, I found myself juggling conflicting instincts about digital mental health before I wrote this Guide. On one side, the worry and sense of unease about how much time children and young people are spending online and the kinds of pressures, trends or even harms that they may be exposed to. On the other hand, I work in scaling and spreading digital and AI mental health innovations which provide powerful tools to support mental health by helping enable early detection, diagnosis and personalised and more accessible interventions. I also realise that for many children and young people, screens offer children a connection, friendship, curiosity, identity as well as a platform for positive learning and entertainment.

In 2024 I conducted a survey and ran workshops with over 450 parents, carers and professionals and over 150 children and young people to explore their insights on children's digital mental health and help inform what priority areas should be included within the book. I was humbled by not only their honesty and transparency, but also their passion to share their tips, ideas and experiences of how to support their peers to promote positive children's digital mental health. The perspectives of parents and professionals are not just referenced in the book, their voices are embedded throughout. Whether it is a parent navigating digital dilemmas at home or a professional offering insight from the classroom or clinic, their contributions deepen the guide's resonance and reflect the realities faced by many families, educators and other professionals.

The motivation to write this guide grew out of personal necessity and professional curiosity. As a parent and as a Children's Digital

Consultant who actively promotes digital wellbeing through delivering, commissioning and scaling innovative digital solutions, I often find myself searching for information, evidence and practical resources and solutions. The insights from parents, professionals and young people are not just powerful - they are transformative. They remind us all that behind every piece of research, academic paper and policy are real families, children and professionals trying to make sense of a digital landscape that often feels challenging and overwhelming.

This guide blends both research and current data, information and expert insight alongside helpful hints, practical tools and engaging activities to help support both you and your child thrive online. Whether you are starting from a place of uncertainty or seek to deepen your understanding of children's digital mental health, I hope that this guide provides you with tools to help you support your child thrive online in an ever-changing digital world.

Section 1: Introduction

Chapter 1:
Introduction

Key facts

- Over a third of 3- to 5-year-olds use social media.
- 66% of 3- to 17-year-olds watch live stream videos.
- 9 out of 10 children own their own phone by the time they are 11 years old.
- Almost 3/4 of teenagers between the age of 13 and 17 have encountered one or more potential harms online.
- 3 out of 5 secondary school children have been contacted online in a way that potentially made them feel uncomfortable.
- A third of children are spending an average of 35 hours per week online (Policy Exchange, 2024)

(Unless separately referenced, all statistics are from Ofcom 2024 and 2025.)

The online world at their fingertips: The digital lives of children and young people

The online world is at the fingertips of children and young people today, through the widespread access to smartphones, the internet and social media platforms. According to Ofcom, 97% of children aged between 0 and 18 years old have internet access through a phone or computer. The 5Rights Foundation states that the daily average screen time of a 13- to 18-year-old is 8 hours 39 minutes. What is more, children are also accessing online devices at an earlier and earlier age. Ofcom has found that nearly three quarters of 5- to 7-year-olds own a smartphone and 76% have access to a tablet.

Access to the digital world poses many social, emotional and educational benefits for us all, especially for children and young people. From following popular trends on social media, connecting with friends and family, to learning new cultures and accessing mental health support online, children and young people are more informed, digitally savvy and technologically astute than ever before. However, access to the digital world can also have a significant impact on children and young people's mental wellbeing in a detrimental way through excessive screentime and usage, cyber bullying, over attachment to digital devices and exposure to harmful and upsetting content online.

In their words: Insights from parents, carers and professionals on digital mental health

More than 450 parents, carers and professionals shared their insights on children and young people's digital mental health which influenced which priority areas were covered within each chapter. They were asked about their concerns on children and young people's online use, and about the key barriers to children's mental wellbeing as a result of their digital use. They were also asked to share some of the practical tips which they thought were useful to help support the digital mental health of children and young people. These insights and ideas for practical tips have been embedded throughout the Guide and have provided a valuable and rich perspective and experience. From those who were consulted, the majority of parents, carers and professionals (79%) were concerned about children and young people's digital mental health with many expressing that they didn't have the digital literacy skills to help, and called for better regulations from tech companies. They shared that they were concerned about online harms especially pornographic, racist and misogynistic content, cyberbullying and the focus on negative body image content online, especially through social media.

In their words: Insights from children and young people on digital mental health

Children and young people were also consulted and offered valuable perspectives on the benefits and risks from their engagement in the online world. They tended to embrace their online world and the positive opportunities it provided to socially connect with friends and family through gaming and social media, for fun, relaxation and entertainment, to learn new things and to be creative and promote self-expression and to help with their mental health. However, they were also observed the risks that it brought, including privacy and online safety concerns; being exposed to violent, sexual and negative content; fake news and misinformation; pressures to look and be perfect, and becoming addicted through overuse. They also shared their valuable perspectives on what support from parents, carers and professionals would help them thrive better online which are shared within this guide.

How to navigate this guide

This *A to Z Guide on Children and Young People's Digital Mental Health* is aimed at parents, carers, educators and professionals and provides a practical approach through activities and tips which can be used in the home, clinical or school/college setting. This easily accessible book is one that you can dip in and out of, according to your area of interest but, most importantly, it provides a number of activities that you may wish to explore together with your child to support their digital resilience. The tips and activities within the guide should be implemented by considering the child's age and maturity.

The book uses a trauma-informed approach in terms of children and young people's use of technology but in particular, with reference to online safety. It reinforces the need to ensure that all tools, sites, platforms, apps and devices promote healing, support and empowerment, and prioritise emotional and psychological wellbeing. It highlights the importance of encouraging supportive and positive interactions to ensure children feel safe, heard and understood by providing psychologically safe spaces – not only with those who work with children and young people but also parents and professionals themselves. By embedding a trauma-informed approach, the activities shared within the book will help parents and professionals explore safe ways to use digital devices with their children and help create choices of online use, help build resilience and instil a sense of connection and trust.

Being a digitally resilient parent, carer or professional means equipping yourself and your child with the right skills to navigate the online world safely and responsibly. This Guide shows that it is important to have regular conversations with your child to help build healthy, lifelong digital habits. It helps to be able to normalise these conversations about both their negative and positive online experiences by listening with empathy, openness and digital resilience. Digital parenting is about modelling responsible digital behaviour yourself, by demonstrating kindness, respect and critical thinking in any digital interaction. It is also about being able to understand the online world that your child is navigating; being able to recognise the risks without feeling overwhelmed with fear or denial is imperative.

This Guide is made up of different chapters based on the alphabet and chosen through consultation with professionals, children and their families. Some chapters are more detailed than others. All the names of contributors to the book have been removed and made anonymous to ensure confidentiality throughout the Guide. Details of specific influencers have been kept to a minimum, because, whilst most promote positive messages, there are those who do not and this can have a significant negative impact on the mental health and wellbeing of the children and young people who view them. Therefore, it is important to resist signposting to specific influencers, whose popularity comes and goes, with the aim of not adding to their likes or following.

References

Policy Exchange (2024) *'Disconnect: The case for a smartphone ban in schools'* London: Policy Exchange - https://policyexchange.org.uk/publication/disconnect/

Ofcom (2024, 19 April) *'A window into young children's online worlds'*, Ofcom, www.ofcom.org.uk.

Ofcom (2024, 6 February) *'How the Online Safety Act will help protect children'*, Ofcom, www.ofcom.org.uk

5Rights Foundation – 5Rightsfoundation.com

Ofcom (2025, 7 May) *'Children and parents: media use and attitudes report'*, Ofcom, www.ofcom.org.uk

Chapter 2:

Children's mental health in an online world

The chapter will cover:

- An overview of children's digital use and how it drives human behaviour.
- The mental health of children and young people globally and in the UK.
- The impact of social media on children and young people's mental health.
- A summary of the benefits and risks of online use and children and young people's mental health.

Introduction

With children and young people glued more and more to their screens and spending more and more time in their online world, should we be worried about whether this affects their mental health? We are aware of the postive impact of being online which allows children to learn, create and socialise with others. However, there is growing evidence that suggests excessive digital use – exposure to online harmful content including misogyny, racism, unrealistic body ideals and the potential for online bullying – has an effect on children and young people's physical and mental wellbeing.

Adolescence is a crucial period for young people developing social and emotional habits which is key for their mental wellbeing. Excessive online use and exposure to online harm, or negative and harmful content, will have a detrimental effect on their mental health.

How digital use meets or affects different levels of children and young people's needs

American psychologist Abraham Maslow developed what he called a 'Hierarchy of Need' (1943), explaining human need in the form of a pyramid which explained the components necessary for a person to have their physical, mental and social needs fully met. This pyramid can be adapted to understand children and young people's digital use and needs. The 'hierarchy of need' below has been adapted from Maslow's to reflect the different elements of engagement in online activity, and how it drives human behaviour. It is illustrated in a pyramid which, like Maslow's, places physiological needs at the base of the pyramid which is considered the most important basic need for engaging in online activities, and self-actualisation portrayed as the ultimate need at the top of the pyramid. The needs are key aspects of what motivates individuals whilst engaging in digital spaces.

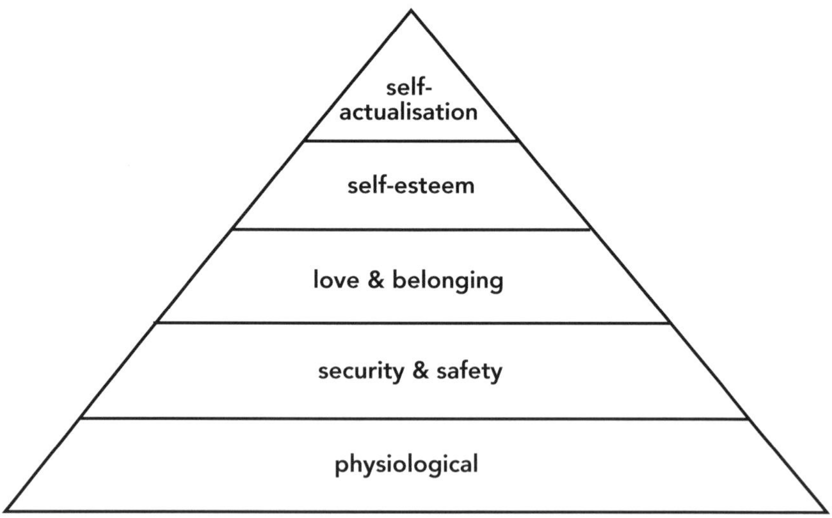

Figure 1: A digital hierarchy of needs (adapted from Maslow's Hierarchy of Need, 1943)

The different layers of the pyramid define different human needs linked to the engagement of online activity.

- **Physiological needs** is a basic need and refers to access to technology e.g. the need for WiFi connection, equipment, software, data and storage, electricity and batteries to power devices.
- **Security and safety** are also basic needs and refers to the importance of online saftey, access to privacy and protection, use of parental controls and implementation of safety regulations to prevent exposure to online harmful content.
- **Love and belonging** are psychological needs; this includes online social interaction through collaboration and connection with friends and family. It refers to friendships and access to online communities and the importance of a sense of belonging.
- **Self-esteem** is another psychological need and hightlights the need for respect, validation and feeling valued when engaging in online activities (e.g. through social media likes or ranking in a game). It includes not only the admiration and respect of others but self respect and self confidence.
- **Self-actualisation** refers to the need to maximise one's full potential online through creative self-expression, active digital identity and digital literacy and ultimately positive digital mental wellbeing.

The mental health of children and young people

We know that more and more children and young people are struggling with their mental health. The World Health Organisation (2024) has found that one in seven 10 to 19 year olds experience a mental health disorder. This accounts for 15% of the global burden of disease amongst this age group; for many, their mental ill-health remains unrecognised or untreated. The main causes of illness and disability amongst this age group are anxiety, depression and behavioural disorders (WHO, 2024). Many mental illnesses experienced in adulthood have their roots in adolescence which is a critical period of brain development and emotional growth. The use of digital spaces during adolescence – including exposure to cyberbullying, online harms, unrealistic social and body comparisons – can contribute to the onset of conditions such as anxiety, depression and psychosis.

Current data in the UK shows that one in five 8 to 25 year olds will have had a probable mental health disorder (NHS Digital, 2023). The Children's Commissioner (2025) in her report "Children's mental health services 2023-2024" states that children are waiting too long to access the help they need, with children waiting on average for 6 months for treatment to begin and almost a third of these waiting for over a year.

The impact of social media and children and young people's mental health

In his book '*The Anxious Generation*' (2024), James Haidt discusses the ways in which social media has had an impact on children and young people's mental health. He says that the rise of Smartphone-based childhoods has contributed to an epidemic of depression and anxiety with excessive online use leading to the rewiring of the adolescent brain. Haidt notes that Gen Z (i.e. children born since1997), who have grown up with access to smartphones and constant online connectivity have been subjected to a range of mental health problems. He warns that social media platforms are designed for engagement rather than mental wellbeing. Haidt advocates for stricter regulations for children and young people on social media use and delaying their access to smartphones until later adolesence, instead, promoting access to more offline activities away from screens.

Positive impact of online use and mental wellbeing

When online platforms are used responsibly, safely and in moderation, there are some fundamental benefits to children and young people's mental wellbeing. For example:

✔ **To connect with others** – from speaking with others through gaming to chatting through social media, digital technology is a great way to interact and make new friends, and stay connected with friends and family. It is especially important for those who struggle to make friends face to face or feel isolated. It also provides a forum to build communities with like-minded peers who share the same interests. Being able to connect with others online can promote feelings of self-esteem, self-worth and belonging which can have a positive impact on children and young people's mental health.

- ✔ **To learn** – from learning about new topics to helping with homework, digital media can offer a range of opportunities to build skills and develop digital literacy. Being online also helps children build digital skills and familiarity with technology where online communication, research and collaboration are a pre-requisite for most careers.
- ✔ **For creativity and self-expression** – online platforms can provide an opportunity for children and young people to express themselves through creativity by using music, videos or art. It is a way of exploring different interests and hobbies. It offers a place for them to share their thoughts and feelings and express their identities, which can help reinforce their emotional resilience and self-esteem.
- ✔ **Provides access to information, advice and support for mental wellbeing services** – digital media provides a wealth of generic and bespoke information and advice on topics that promote positive mental health and emotional resilience. It also provides mental health support through online interventions and services.
- ✔ **Develop social awareness** – by providing new ideas on global issues and learning about how others live across the world can foster a sense of purpose and meaning which can lead to positive mental wellbeing.
- ✔ **Enhances digital literacy** – by helping children and young people navigate the online world safely and confidently, building skills to recognise online harms and promote healthy digital boundaries.

Negative impact of online use and mental wellbeing

The impact that online use has on children and young people depends on what they are looking at or are exposed to, and how much time they spend online. Many of these examples and strategies to help children and young people develop healthy online habits are discussed in more detail within this Guide. Examples of the negative impact on a child's mental health include, for example:

- ✘ **Body image and appearance issues** – being exposed to edited and filtered images can have a negative effect on appearance concerns and body image as children and young people can strive for a perfect body ideal. This can lead to body comparison and feelings of anxiety and depression.
- ✘ **Feelings of loneliness and social isolation** – over-reliance on screens can lead to some children and young people avoiding face to face interactions which can lead to loneliness and feelings of social isolation.

- ✗ **Exposure to online harms** – **c**hildren and young people can be exposed to inappropriate and harmful content such as cyberbullying, sextortion, grooming, scams and fraud, misogyny, and racism which can lead to feelings of stress, anxiety and depression.
- ✗ **Excessive use** – can lead to concentration difficulties, low mood and anxiety.
- ✗ **Poor sleep** – too much screen time can affect levels of concentration, and cause irritability and low mood.

In today's digital world, children are growing up surrounded by technology that can significantly impact their mental health. As a parent or professional, navigating this landscape can feel overwhelming and exhausting. This *A to Z Guide on Children and Young People's Digital Mental Health* is designed to empower parents and professionals with clear, practical information and strategies for supporting their children's wellbeing in the digital age. From understanding anxiety triggered by social media to setting healthy screen time boundaries, this Guide covers essential topics alphabetically, offering insights, tips, practical activities and resources to help you foster a balanced, safe, and mentally healthy digital environment for you and your child.

References

Boniel-Nissim, M., Marino, C., Galeotti, T., Blinka, L., Ozoliņa, K. *et al.* (2024) *A Focus on Adolescent Social Media Use and Gaming in Europe, Central Asia and Canada: Health behaviour in school-aged children. International report from the 2021/2022 survey.* World Health Organization. Regional Office for Europe.

Boniel-Nissim, M., van den Eijnden, Regina, J.J.M., Furstova, J., Marino, C., Lahti, H., Inchley, J., Šmigelskas, K., Vieno, A. & Badura, P. (2022) 'International perspectives on social media use among adolescents: implications for mental and social wellbeing and substance use', *Computers in Human Behavior*, 129, 107144.

Children's Commissioner (18 May 2025) *"Children's mental health services 2023-2024"*.

Haidt, J. (2024) *The Anxious Generation: How the great rewiring of childhood is causing an epidemic of mental illness*. Allen Lane.

Adapted from the Heirarchy of Technology by Gerstein, J. Originally adapted from Maslow, A. H. (1943). A theory of human motivation. *Psychological Review, 50*(4), 370–396.

NHS (2023) *NHS Digital Survey 2023*. London: NHS.

NHS Digital (2024) *Mental Health Bulletin 2023–2024 Annual Report*. NHS Digital, NHSE.

WHO (2024) *Global Burden of Diseases*. WHO: Institute of Health Metrics and Evaluation.

Chapter 3:
Digital Parenting in a Digital Age

The chapter will cover:

- What digital parenting means.
- The different types of digital parents.
- Digital-parenting children at a young age.
- Parental digital role-modelling.
- Practical tips on digital parenting.

What is digital parenting?

Being a digital parent can be complex and challenging, but we all play a key role in helping to ensure children and young people engage with digital technology both safely and responsibly, in order to thrive in the online world. A digital parent is someone who can guide a child's interaction with digital technology, including setting boundaries and rules for devices, helping educate children about good digital citizenship and online safety, and helping them think critically about their online use.

What type of digital parent are you?

There are many different parenting styles which help children navigate the online world whether it is through social media, gaming or using their smartphones. The digital parenting style used will depend on various factors including a parent's digital literacy, their online experience and cultural values, and the age of a child and the parent (adapted from "Traditional Parenting Styles" within the Council of Europe's "Parenting in the Digital Age").

What type of digital parenting do you recognise?

Types of digital parenting	Digital parenting characteristics	Potential impact
Strict digital parenting	Strict monitoring and restrictive rules with limited explanation or discussions about the impact. Limited input from a child in conversations.	Could lead to hidden secretive online behaviours.
Authoritative digital parenting	Sets rules and boundaries in consultation with a child through conversations with them.	Can lead to better self-regulation of online use.
Laidback digital parenting	Few rules or boundaries about digital rules or boundaries. A child's digital use will often be based on trust.	Could lead to over-exposure of digital content and poor online self-regulation.
Arms-length digital parenting	Little or no involvement in a child's online world which may be due to lack of digital literacy or interest. This relies on a child being able to/ having to self-regulate their own online use.	Could lead to over-exposure of digital content and poor online self-regulation.

Engaged digital parenting	Active engagement where digital use is shared together (e.g. playing games together) which helps foster engagement.	Can build parent and child digital literacy and helps develop safe digital habits.

Whilst the different styles of parenting have merits and challenges, parents will often use a variety of digital parenting approaches depending on their individual child, and the age of a child. What is most important about digital parenting is maintaining open and honest communication with your child, providing them a space where they feel safe and comfortable to discuss their online concerns without feeling judged or blamed. This Guide provides practical tools and tips to help you to digitally-parent confidently and positively and offers conversation starters which will allow you to begin and maintain discussions with your child.

Digital parenting children at a young age

Children are accessing digital technology at an earlier and earlier age. Whilst children have been exposed to screens, especially the television, for many years, screen exposure through the use of a smartphone or iPad starts at a very young age. In the "*Children and Parents: Media Use and Attitudes Report*" (2025), Ofcom found that 19% of 3- to 5-year-olds have their own mobile phone with 31% playing games online and 19% using social platforms unsupervised. The report also stated that one in three 5- to 7-year-olds use social media independently, with 41% playing online games. Ofcom's report "*A window into young children's online worlds*" (2024) states that by the age of 5 to 7 years old over, nearly a third (30%) of children own their own smartphone with 38% of children this age accessing social media platforms, despite platforms having a minimum age restriction of 13 years old. For parents, screens can be used as a convenient digital babysitter, by helping keep our children occupied or entertained whilst we engage with everyday household tasks and at work. How often are very young children offered the use of a screen to keep them entertained and occupied whilst in the car, at the supermarket or whilst eating out?

Whilst the use of technology can have educational and cognitive benefits, there are many implications on a child's healthy developmental and behaviour when introduced so early in their lives. Youvan (2024) states that excessive screen time in pre-school aged children is linked to increased aggression and hyperactivity, as well as depression and anxiety. With screens replacing face to face interaction and play, behavioural issues are exacerbated with impacts on emotional and social development. It is important to promote mindful screen use from a very early age by encouraging offline interactive activities that promote healthy behaviour and development of children at a young age, rather than a reliance on screens.

Digital parenting role models

Whilst it is easy to comment on our children's excessive use of online devices, it is also important to consider our own screen use! Is it easy to prioritise scrolling through endless feeds on social media rather than reading a bedtime story? Research in Australia (Toledo-Vargas, 2025) found that parents who frequently used technology around their children led to their child's poorer cognitive and social development, reduced emotional attachment and increased behavioural problems. Technoference refers to the everyday interruptions in interpersonal interactions caused by the preoccupation in digital devices. If parents are constantly distracted by their own phones, they miss opportunities for connection with their child or being present especially at key times during the day e.g. mealtimes, bedtimes or when playing. It is important for parents to promote themselves as a heathy digital role model through their own digital habits to help promote positive mental wellbeing.

Practical tips on digital parenting

Whilst this Guide provides several practical tips and activities to help you navigate your role as a digital parent, here are some reminders to help you thrive:

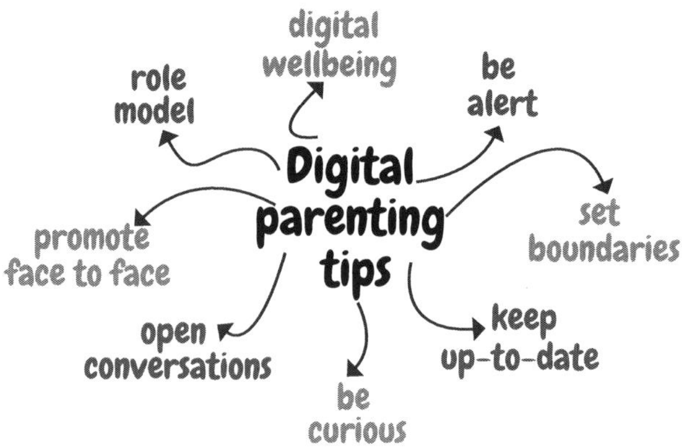

Figure 2: Tips for digital parenting

- **Be a good digital role model** – it is important to consider critically how we interact with digital technology ourselves, and do more to promote a positive role model for our children of healthy digital habits. Balance your own screentime!
- **Promote interactive face to face activities** to support the healthy development and promote positive behaviours. Encourage children to engage with activities away from their screens.
- **Talk to your child about their online experiences** – engage in open and honest conversations regularly so that your child will talk about their online experiences and concerns. Try and encourage conversations without fear of being punished or judged. Start age-appropriate conversations early.
- Try and **understand the online world your child is engaging with** – be curious and interested but not critical. Keep up to date with what types of games your child is playing online, who they are talking too through social media, what social media apps they are using and why.
- Work together to set age-appropriate **boundaries and controls** together. Use parental controls and adjust privacy settings based on your child's age.
- Stay alert to the potentials of **online harms** by knowing what content your child is accessing online and who they are interacting with.
- **Educate yourself** about current apps, platforms and online trends.
- Focus on **digital wellbeing** by encouraging them to use digital spaces that are safe and make them feel happy not anxious, left out or unhappy.

For more information and advice

UNICEF provides information and resources on digital parenting – https://www.unicef.org/parenting/digital-parenting

References

Youvan, C. (2024) 'The impact of screen time on early childhood development: a comprehensive review of health guidelines and research findings'. DOI: 10.13140/RG.2.2.22151.41127. September 2024.

"A window into young children's online worlds". Ofcom. (19 April 2024).

"Children and Parent: Media Use and Attitudes Report". Ofcom.

"Children and Parents: Media Use and Attitudes Report". Ofcom. (7 May 2025).

Toledo-Vargas, M. (2025) 'Parental technology use in a child's presence and health and development in the early years: a systematic review and meta analysis'. JAMA Pediatrics.

Milovidov, E. (2020) 'Parenting in the digital age: positive parenting strategies for different scenarios', Council of Europe. p.12. (https://rm.coe.int/publication-parenting-in-the-digital-age-2020-eng/1680a0855a).

Chapter 4:

Parents, Carers and Professionals – Views and Practical Tips

This chapter will consider parents, carers and professionals' views on:

- How they feel about children and young people using online platforms, including social media and gaming.
- How they think it positively supports – and negatively affects – their child's mental wellbeing.
- An overview of practical 'top tips' to support children and young people's mental health.

Introduction

More than 400 parents, educators and practitioners were consulted through a survey undertaken by the author (Randell, 2025), through either one-to-one interviews or focus groups to provide insight into the digital mental health of children and young people. They were asked how they felt about children and young people's use of online platforms, their views about the positives and negatives of digital use to children and young people's mental wellbeing and to share their tips for other parents and professionals. Their voices are powerful and insightful and embedded throughout this *A to Z Guide to Children's Digital Mental Health.*

A survey to understand more about digital mental health was completed by 287 parents and professionals during Autumn 2024. Responses were received by 43% parents (n = 102), 35% practitioners or clinicians (n = 85), 15% educators (n = 36) and 7% others (n = 17). Other professionals included social workers, academics and youth workers.

Parents, carers and professionals' views

How they feel about children and young people's use of online platforms (including social media and gaming)

Four out of every five parents, educators and practitioners were either slightly concerned (46%) or very concerned (33%) about children and young people's use of online platforms, including social media and gaming. Only 12% said that they were felt ok about children and young people's online use and only 1% (n = 2) felt positive about their use of online platforms.

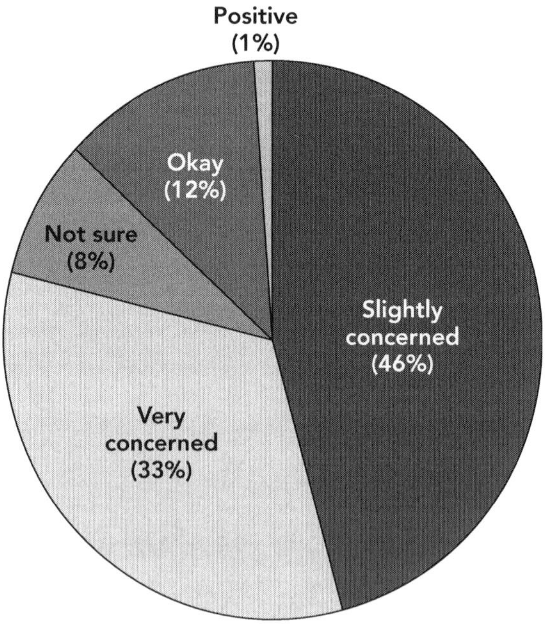

Figure 3: Parents, educators and practitioners' views of children's use of online platforms

Even of those parents, educators and practitioners who stated that they were very or slightly concerned about children and young people's use of online platforms, many also identified the positive opportunities. For example, one parent said:

"There are a lot of benefits ... meeting peers......positive way to help you deal with your mental health".

Another talked about the opportunities for:

"learning and accessing educational resources" and "with access to the right apps which offer good support, it can be a social outlet for many children who are lonely and isolated".

Educators mentioned the importance of social media for connectedness, providing coping strategies and helping reduce the negative stigma of mental health. Practitioners reflected on the availability of access to online interventions and resources to support children's emotional wellbeing, resilience and mental health.

A large number of parents (79%) said that they were either very or slightly concerned and identified the key issues being: online safety; time spent online; impact on mental health; exposure to risky, harmful, and inappropriate content; bullying online; the excessive use and addictive nature of social media; and their lack of knowledge or skills in being able to support their child.

One parent reflected that:

"the material that they can access is damaging and I cannot control their access and feel it is ruining their innocence and the perception of themselves".

Another parent reflected that:

> *"my daughter has a very obsessive personality, so I worry about how these digital platforms impact on her mental health and how it potentially allows her access to people and content that isn't appropriate for her".*

Parents also noted the lack of regulation by technology firms, one parent noting that:

> *"because content isn't regulated and there are no standards applied. It's an enormous task to manage what they are watching and not realistic, so I'm left hoping the boundaries I have put in place (both using the apps and verbal) are good enough".*

Practitioners and educators who were very or slightly concerned identified the reasons as being lack of parental controls, lack of regulation, children and young people's access to phones and harmful online contents. One practitioner noted that:

> *"I am concerned on a number of levels about how technology affects children's mental health. This includes the re-wiring of children's brains, how it affects their sleep, their attention spans, their ability to complete tasks and the impact it has on their socialisation skills".*

Another practitioner stated that:

> *"daily I hear from children and young people about how their online use affects their self-esteem and anxiety levels".*

A teacher noted that:

> *"it feels like we are conducting an experiment with a whole generation of children. I am concerned about the lack of regulation and responsibility for any of us of any age using some of these platforms".*

How can digital platforms and technology support children's mental health?

Professionals identified how digital platforms could support as a learning tool as well as providing information and advice on a range of mental health concerns. Practitioners highlighted how online interventions supported children's mental health especially online interventions and apps. One practitioner said:

> *"young people are used to technology and often prefer to access support this way, so it increases accessibility.... and is available instantly".*

Professionals also shared how technology could support coping strategies and help reduce the stigma of mental health.

Parents were less positive than practitioners and educators about how digital platforms and technology could support children and young people's mental health. Many parents highlighted that they were "unsure" how they could help. Some parents noted that there were several apps or websites that provided children with support, information and guidance on mental wellbeing.

Parents and professionals reflected that online platforms and social media could be a positive way for children to meet, connect and socialise with friends and peers.

A teacher noted that:

> *"Online platforms can be safe spaces to communicate, play, create and share with friends. Online friendships can be just as socially rewarding as in person friendships and can be platforms for children to meet like-minded others with similar interests that they may not find in their schools. I have worked with students who felt like social outcasts within their peer groups at school but have made meaningful friendships gaming online or at meet-ups about a particular interest of theirs they found out about on online forums. Children have more access to help than ever thanks to online accessibility, whether it be helplines and mental health services or spaces for them to feel heard and seen. It can be a space for young people questioning their sexuality or identity to safely discover and relate to identities they may not have the chance to learn about in their setting, which can help with self-worth and self-esteem. For children with disabilities, the world is far more accessible to them than previous generations thanks to technological support and innovation".*

Top tips on how to better support children's use of digital technology

Parents, practitioners and educators were asked for their top tips on how to better support children and young people's use of digital technology and many of these suggestions and helpful hints have been embedded within this Guide.

An overview of the themes of the practical tips are listed on p.27.

- **Communication –** engage in open and honest dialogue and regular conversations.
- **Access –** monitor and restrict/limit time and usage; have regular checks of accounts and what is being accessed and with whom; clear and healthy boundaries and parental controls; use of safeguards; consider age of use of smartphones and access to social media and digital breaks and detox.
- **Approach –** take an interest in what children and young people are accessing and doing online; promote alternative (offline) activities; be curious and non-judgemental, building trust and respect; lead by example as a role model; recognise warning signs to spot signs of digital distress.
- **Digital literacy –** build on digital literacy skills and knowledge; seek education on online safety and be aware of risks; keep up to date with technology and encourage children to think critically about what they see and do online.

Chapter 5:

What support do children and young people want?

The chapter will cover:

- An overview of both the positive and negative impact of an online world.
- Views of children and young people on how they want to be supported to navigate their online world.
- Practical tips that children and young people want parents, carers and professionals to follow.

Children and young people's positive impact of their online world

Children and young people have identified several positive things that impact on their online world from connecting with friends, family and peers; entertainment, relaxation and fun; learning new things; being creative and promoting self-expression, and to help their mental wellbeing.

Children and young people's negative impact of their online world

Whilst children and young people recognise several benefits of being online, they have also identified many negative impacts. For example, privacy and online safety concerns; being exposed to violent, sexual and negative content; fake news and misinformation; pressures to look and be 'perfect', and being addicted through overuse.

Views of children and young people

More than 150 children and young people from the age of 8 to 24 were consulted and they offered insight about their online lives (Randell, 2025). This included advice to parents, carers and professionals about what support they needed to help them navigate their online world. These have been embedded throughout this Guide and helped influence the range of practical tips and activities.

Examples of some of the feedback that we received from children and young people which have been themed include:

- **Digital social lives – online spaces are the places where children and young people interact and meet friends.**

> *"Our social lives are online – when my mum tells me she is worried because I have no friends. It upsets me, I do have friends, lots of friends … they are online, that is where I meet them", "being on my phone helps me feel included and liked" and "finding people with similar interests as you and staying in contact with them even if you don't have the time and energy to see them and meet up… helps maintain friendships".*

- **Parental controls – age-appropriate supportive boundaries can help create safer online experiences.**

> *"I know more than my parents about how they (devices) work. I know how to get round the parental controls!"*

- **Self-regulation and feeling empowered to control their engagement with online spaces.**

> *"I can regulate my online use myself. I set myself timers or time limits. It is about trusting young people because they often know more than their parents about how to manage their own online use".*

"We need to be empowered more to take responsibility of how and what we use"

- **Open communication – can promote discussions and positive healthy digital conversations and create a space that children and young people can access if they are worried about something online.**

"It would help if they talked to me about why I can't have a phone. All my friends have a phone. They don't realise that because I don't have a phone I don't know what is going on with my friends".

"My mum is always happy to talk to me if I am worried about stuff online"

"It is important to initiate conversations and ask about your child's online world, like you would ask about school or what kind of day they have had – ask about their online world".

"If a young person makes a mistake or shares something they shouldn't, they need the parent's support and not fear they will be in trouble".

- **Banning and restricting phones is often seen as a way of shutting down conversations about online use by some but an opportunity to help keep others safe.**

"Our school has tried to ban phones to stop us spending too much time online but then sets us homework online and if we have no phone, we can't access school portal to know what has been set!" and "by taking my phone away as a punishment doesn't help because I find a way to use my phone secretly and they never know that I am on it".

"There should be rules about restricting access to social media but bear in mind that children have different ages of maturity".

"Don't just ban me ... explain why."

- **Digital literacy of parents, carers and professionals can help understand what the risks are and support and understand the online world that children occupy.**

"We want adults to understand our online world better!"

"They don't have a clue ... they think it's all about rules but if they tried to find out more about what was available online and the pressure we have online, it might help".

"If adults explain things rather just telling us now what to do or look at, it would really help".

- **Digital role models – parents, carers and professionals need to lead by example and model positive digital behaviour.**

"My parents are always telling me to get off my phone, but they are always on theirs – it's double standards!"

"If they are always on their phones we will be too".

- **Sharenting – oversharing of personal information, videos and photographs can result in children and young people feeling over exposed, awkward and uncomfortable.**

"I can't believe my dad posts pictures of me on Facebook.... it's embarrassing and he thinks it's ok!"

"Posting pictures of your kids online is not OK.... their friends can see it and it's there forever.... It is a big NO!"

"They wouldn't like it if I posted photos of them on holiday".

- **Online safety – to receive up to date and current age-appropriate help with online safety.**

"We know a lot about online safety but we need help with the real problems about being online".

"The online safety help we get at school is out of date, we know more than the teachers"

"It is important to make sure really young kids get online safety support before they come across bad stuff online".

Practical TIPS Practical tips that children and young people want parents, carers and professionals to follow

Children and young people identified a number of ways that they wanted parents and professionals to support them, including:

- **To be listened to and heard –** want to feel safe and not judged when they are worried about things they see or hear online. Want to feel that they can talk about their concerns without being judged.
- **Trusted and respected** – working with them to agree what the boundaries should be and reviewing them regularly together.
- **Tools and help to help them stay safe online,** protect identity and be able to spot fake news. Children and young people acknowledged that they received information about online safety especially through school but wanted more detailed information.
- **Respect of their privacy** by trusting their child's online use and not 'being spied on' or 'tracked'.

- **Offering help when and if things go wrong** by being open to conversations and not judging.
- **Understand that being online is their social life** and online friendships or communities can be meaningful and support mental wellbeing.
- **Knowing more about the online world** by parents equipping themselves with the knowledge and skills of what is available and current trends online and what children and young people are accessing.
- **Lead by example** by being a digital role model. Children and young people notice if parents ignore their own digital rules so need to practise what they preach!

Section 2: The A-Z Guide

A – Artificial Intelligence (AI)

The chapter will cover:

- Overview of research and artificial intelligence.
- How artificial intelligence can be used to enhance mental health.
- Opportunities and risks of artificial intelligence.
- Chatbots and chat companions.
- Views of parents, carers and professionals on digital wellbeing using AI.
- Practical tips and activities on helping children and young people navigate the world of AI.

What about AI?

Artificial Intelligence (AI) is deeply embedded within our everyday lives, often in ways that we do not even realise. AI has a key role, from asking Alexa to play calming music or tell a joke to providing chatbots for emotional support, and helping with a child's homework. AI is about creating intelligent machines which think and learn like humans. AI has many roles, for example, it can process information, make decisions, and adapt to new situations to perform tasks that would typically require human input. AI functions can include for example, recognising speech, translating language or recognising images, having a conversation, solving problems, finding information or gaming. AI is part of our everyday digital world and is being seen by many people as one of the key ways to support the transformation of mental health.

What does the research say about children and young people and AI?

AI is a key element of children and young people's digital lives especially for learning and social connection. Ofcom (2024) found that children and young people were twice as likely as adults to use AI. In fact, one in four adults did not know what AI was, and over two thirds (69%) of adults implied that they had never used it. Half of children state that they use AI tools (Ofcom, 2025) and more children are using AI to learn or at school.

However, young people who use AI hold differing opinions on whether to trust it or not.

- Over a third (36%) of AI users aged between 13 and 17 say that they would trust an AI-generated news story less than one written by a human.
- A similar number of young people (35%) say that they would trust it to the same extent as the human version.
- Only 17% would trust an AI-generated news story more than one written by a human.

"Children's Media Literacy Report" (Ofcom, 2025)

However, children and adults both identified apprehension about the use of AI in their daily lives. Ofcom (2024) found that nearly half of children and young people shared that they were worried about the future impact of generative AI. Similar concerns were shared by adults about the impact of AI on the reliability of information, misinformation and its societal impact.

How AI can be used to enhance mental wellbeing

With the continuous advancement of technology and innovation, AI plays a key role in our digital world to support children and young people's mental health and wellbeing. Listed below are some examples of how AI can be used to enhance mental wellbeing.

- **Early intervention and detection** – AI algorithms and reviewing data patterns through AI can help the detection of those at risk of developing mental health issues.
- **Social and emotional learning** – there are a number of AI solutions that help children and young people's social and emotional learning either at home or in the classroom. AI solutions can be a helpful tool

to provide tailored support to those children with special educational needs and those who have severe difficulties attending school due to their emotional wellbeing.

- **Personalised care and clinical support** – AI can tailor mental health interventions based on analysing an individual's need, what they prefer and their behaviour. For example, virtual therapeutic solutions using AI technology can potentially provide personalised care by stimulating human interactions.
- **Emotional support** – Some helplines are operated through AI. These can offer immediate accessibility and response rates to those who access them. There are also a number of mental health apps which customise emotional support through AI including, for example, programmes to help with sleep, mindfulness and stress management. AI companions can provide a source of emotional support and stimulate conversations by asking questions (see below) often taking the role of virtual friend or professional.
- **AI-enabled wearable devices** which can help track and monitor mental health symptoms and/or physiological data e.g. sleep patterns or mood etc.
- **AI can also create games** to promote mental health awareness and resilience behaviours.
- **AI is used to contribute to the assessment and diagnosis** of mental health issues.

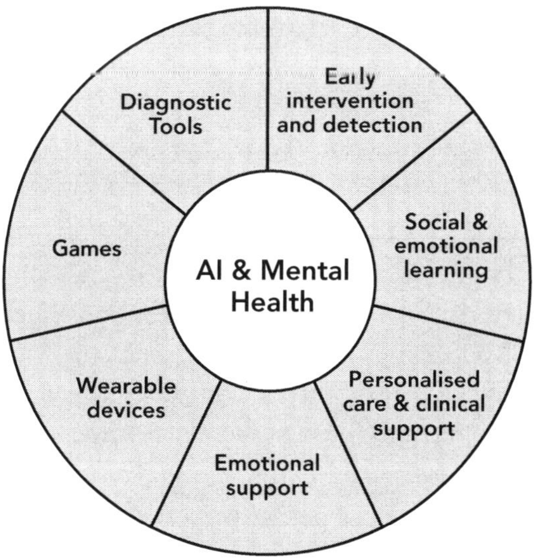

Figure 4: Ways in which AI can support mental wellbeing

Opportunities and challenges of AI and social media

Whilst there are a number of opportunities with AI and social media, there are also some risks that need to be recognised.

Opportunities

AI is playing an increasingly innovative role in supporting children and young people's mental health including, for example:

- AI can **moderate contents** by detecting inappropriate or harmful contents (e.g. cyberbullying, hate speech, misogyny) from social media and remove them from social media.
- AI can **curate contents** by analysing an individual's interests and behaviour online and will then recommend posts, images and information based on individual preferences.
- AI can **facilitate interaction and connectivity** by suggesting friends or communities to link with based on an individual's interests and behaviour online.
- AI chatbots and algorithms can direct individuals to specific **mental health support or resources**.
- AI tools can **improve accessibility** by providing automated captions, translations and voice assistants features which help to make social media more inclusive for those with disabilities, or where English is not the first language.

Risks

Whilst AI can help and support children and young people's mental health, it is also important to recognise that it has a number of risks and limitations. For example:

- **Algorithm bias** can result in unintentionally reinforcing societal biases, discrimination and stereotypes by recommending specific contents. It can also amplify online harmful contents through engagement-driven contents (e.g. hate speech, fake news or misogyny).
- **Reinforce excessive online use** through AI-powered algorithms which target and personalise social media feeds to make them more addictive and increase engagement.

- If not used properly AI can collect and misuse personal data collects which can lead to **privacy and security concerns**.
- AI can create **echo chambers** which allows us to only see content that aligns with our own views which can reduce our exposure to alternative and new ideas and perspectives. This can be extremely problematic when the opinions are biased, incorrect, hateful or discriminatory.
- Children and young people may **form attachments with AI companions** which may impact on real life relationships and mental wellbeing.
- AI can be used to **scam people** by targeting them with manipulative advertisements.
- Personalised AI-curated feeds can affect **self-esteem and cause anxiety** by encouraging unhealthy comparisons.

Chatbots and chat companions

Parents asked for more information on what chatbots could be used for to support children's mental health and their limitations. Chatbots are used for specific tasks whereas chat companions are built to have more meaningful, human-like behaviour to offer personalised support. Powered by AI they converse using text or spoken word. For some children and young people, they offer access to an immediate and anonymous platform to share their feelings without fear of being judged by another human.

However, they do have risks attached to using them, if not used properly and safely. A lot of AI chatbots are designed by adults and for adults. Whilst chatbots and chat companions use language and words we can relate to, they can be criticised for not being able to deal with the emotional and unpredictable aspect of conversations which can lead to an 'empathy gap' (Kurian, 2023). It is important to make sure that children are accessing **age-appropriate** chatbots to reduce the chance of them accessing harmful or inappropriate contents. It is important to remind your child that whilst chatbots and companions can provide additional mental health information, guidance and support they should **not be considered a replacement for human connection and interaction.**

Views from parents, carers and professionals about AI

Parents and professionals who mentioned AI had specific comments about algorithms and in particular fear and lack of understanding about how AI works. For example, one practitioner noted that:

> *"whilst there are positives, some young people are exposed to harmful content through algorithms that they have no control over".*

and another suggested the need to:

> *"encourage them to engage with positive content – tech works off algorithms, so the more funny dog videos they like the more funny dog videos will show up (in the same way the more upsetting/ distressing contents we engage with, the more shows up…it's not rocket science!)".*

Several parents expressed their concerns, stating that:

> *"the algorithm works for itself, not in your child's best interests";*

and

> *"some of the algorithms increase an individual's access to subjects that are not age or stage appropriate and some that can cause exposure to online harms."*

Practical TIPS: Practical tips on helping children and young people navigate the world of AI

The following practical tips are suggestions for parents and professionals on ways to help children and young people navigate the world of AI safely and responsibly:

- Have **open and honest conversations** about their online experiences and encourage them to share any conversations that cause them to worry with you or a trusted adult. Help your child see some of the benefits of AI – how AI can support learning, creativity and mental wellbeing when used properly. It is important to also discuss the limitations of AI.
- **Educate them on how AI works.** Whilst AI appears to take on the function of a friend or trusted adult, it is important to remind your child that AI systems are not real and don't have feelings in the same way that humans do.
- Review all **privacy settings and parental controls** regarding your child's online use but in particular access to AI tools being used.
- Set **clear boundaries for online use** and reinforce the importance of critical thinking when accessing AI systems online. It is important to remind children and young people that not all information and guidance given through AI is correct.
- Do not hesitate to seek **professional help** if you are concerned about your child's mental health.

Activities

There are many ways to use AI-powered activities within the family or in a classroom setting which can be fun and engaging, subject your accessibility of AI tools. Caution should always be taken with the accuracy of information provided through different AI devices as they draw their responses from a range of different online sources (e.g. ChatGPT, MyAI, Google Gemini or Alexa).

1. Story telling

Ask your child to describe a fictional character and the world in which they live and use AI (e.g. ChatGPT, MyAI, Google Gemini or Alexa) to help you write a story together. The story can be printed and illustrated afterwards!

2. Fun quiz

Ask your child to pick a topic for a quiz (e.g. animals, music or food) and ask your AI device to create a quiz. You can also ask them to create generic age-appropriate general knowledge quizzes.

3. Top wellbeing tips

With your child, use your AI devices to ask for top tips on supporting your child's wellbeing (e.g. "Tell me some tips for getting a good night's sleep" or "Give me a mindfulness exercise")

4. Key facts quiz

Ask your child to pick a topic that they would like to know more about. Ask AI devices to tell you and your child fun facts about that topic to learn more about a specific subject (e.g. "Tell me five fun facts about elephants" or "Tell me the top ten highest mountains")

For more information and advice for parents and practitioners on AI and children's digital mental health:

Internet Matters provides information on chatbots and chat companions:
https://www.internetmatters.org/resources/ai-chatbots-and-virtual-friends-how-parents-can-keep-children-safe/

Internet Matters provides a parent's guide to AI:
https://www.internetmatters.org/resources/parent-guide-to-artificial-intelligence-ai-tools/

References

Kurian, N. (2024) *"No, Alexa, no!" Designing child-safe AI and protecting children from the risks of the 'empathy gap' in large language models*, 10 July 2024, Learning, Media and Technology. (https://www.tandfonline.com/doi/full/10.1080/17439884.2024.2367052).

Ofcom (2024) 'Online Nation', 28 November. Ofcom.

Ofcom (2023) *Ofcom Adult Media Literacy Tracker 2023: Core survey,* Question A8: 'Have you ever used AI models such as ChatGPT or Bard?' (single coded). Ofcom.

Ofcom (2025) "Children's Media Literacy Report" (2025)

B – Body image

The chapter will cover:

- An overview on research on social media and body image.
- The impact of social media on children and young people's body image and appearance.
- Role of social influencers in shaping the perceptions of what children and young people look lik
- Different types of influencers.
- Parents, carers and professionals' views of social media and body image.
- Practical tips and activities on promoting positive body image and appearance

Shaping perception

Social media platforms provide an endless stream of images and content that can shape our perception of both beauty and body ideals. Social media is often seen as responsible for creating a distorted perception of what is perceived as attractive, which consequently can lead to feelings of poor self-esteem, self-doubt and body dissatisfaction. Social media can influence our body image and perceptions of appearance by negatively promoting photo-edited and highly edited images of celebrities, influencers promoting calorie-counting and encouraging the need to compare with others through body checking or the use of filtered images online. However, social media can also promote body positivity and body confidence by showcasing a range of body types and appearances which can challenge unrealistic beauty standards.

What does the research tell us about social media and body image?

Ofcom's 'Online Nation' Report (2024) found differences between teenage girls and boys in relation to body image. The report identified that teenage girls aged 13–17 years-old are more concerned than boys the same age about online content which promoted excessive or unhealthy dieting or exercise (51% girls and 37% boys). The report found that a quarter of girls were more likely than boys (11%) to experience online harms relating to body image including online content that stigmatises body types and eating disorder online content.

Research shows us that children and young people are worried about what they look like when they are online. Internet Matters (2024), through their research of 9 to16 year olds, found that 12% of children were worried about how they look whilst spending time using digital media. More specifically, they found that 15% of boys aged 13 to 14 years old, and 18% of girls aged 15 to 16 years old, identified that they were worried about what they looked like online. The research also identified that 12% of children stated that what they saw online made them worried about their body shape and size, particularly those aged 15 to 16 years old.

For boys too, there appears to be a pursuit of lean and muscular physiques through social media which plays a large part in presenting unrealistic, photo-edited or digitally enhanced images of males. This can often be reinforced through sports and fitness social influencers on social media who promote 'fitspiration' and body transformation challenges which potentially can lead to over training and restrictive dieting. Bell (2024) explores the relationship between social media, body image and the pursuit of muscularity in males. He found that those men who were more active social media users – as defined by liking and commenting on online content – were less satisfied with their bodies and had more negative feelings about what they looked like than those who were less active.

The impact of social media on body image and appearance

Social media can positively present a diverse range of body shapes, weights and sizes which can help promote body positivity and body confidence. However, social media can also lead to children and young people comparing themselves to a **perfect 'body ideal'** or promoting unrealistic beauty standards and appearance. This negative comparison, for some, can have a huge impact on children and young people's self-esteem, self-worth and self-confidence and ultimately affect their mental health.

For many children and young people, they are bombarded online with images of celebrities and social influencers who appear '**body perfect**'. However, often these images can be edited through apps or filters which give a perception of an entirely unrealistic 'perfect body ideal'. With the spread of artificial intelligence, it is easy to adapt and superimpose images. These often-distorted images of celebrities and social influencers can lead to children and young people feeling worse about their own bodies and appearance.

Digital dysmorphia refers to people being fixated on what they look like in digitally altered images online which results in distorted self-perception. There are many ways to edit images through photo-editing and face-tunning apps which can contribute to unrealistic beauty standards and self-perception for children and young people on how they should look. These provide a way for children and young people to create an idealised version of themselves by artificially sculpting the way they look, from changing the colour of their skin and removing blemishes to reducing the size of their nose. The quest for the perfect selfie can result in **'selfie-harm'** through endless digital distortion. If children and young people are feeling less and less confident about themselves and what they look like naturally, they will end up posting more and more altered self-images.

The role of influencers in shaping body image and appearance

Social media influencers play a key role in shaping body image and appearance both negatively and positively. There are those who promote body positivity through diverse body shapes and sizes and challenge the 'body and beauty norm'. Other influencers share their journeys of positive recovery from an eating disorder which can for some people, install hope and support and there are others who promote positive healthy eating tips.

Yet, there are some influencers who reinforce negative messages promoting unrealistic body and beauty standards, which includes edited and enhanced images of themselves. Many influencers will prioritise appearance over health, by prioritising aesthetics over wellbeing. There are others who glorify disordered eating behaviours, for example, calorie counting, 'What I eat in a day' videos or binge eating, restrictive diets and 'cheat' dieting tips. There are influencers who promote overeating and food challenges for entertainment or shock value by eating large quantities of food on camera or competitive eaters (e.g. eating 20 burgers in a day or eating over 10,000 calories a day).

Influencers can also promote body checking behaviours which refers to compulsively scrutinising your own body shape, size and weight in comparison to other bodies portrayed online which are often idealised and give a distorted image of what is real. Continuous body checking can affect self-esteem and self-worth which ultimately impacts on mental wellbeing. Regular body checking can affect algorithms which leads to similar and more of the same feeds creating cycles of body comparison and body checking.

Overview of different types of influencers who can promote both positive and negative body image, unhealthy eating or appearance ideals

There are some influencers who promote positive body image messaging. However, there are others who can also promote negative body image, unhealthy eating and unrealistic beauty ideals which can cause harm, restricting food behaviour and body dysmorphia through their messaging.

Types of influencers	What they promote
Body positivity influencers	Challenge unrealistic beauty standards and body shapes to promote self-acceptance
Fitness and nutrition influencers	Promote healthy eating and physical fitness
Eating disorder recovery influencers	Share personal stories about having had an eating disorder and recovering
Plus size fashion influencers	Promote body confidence no matter your size

Diversity and inclusivity influencers	Promote different body types, ethnicities and abilities to promote inclusive beauty and body shape narratives
Clean eating and wellness influencers	Promote natural, whole food eating and often detoxing
Fitness extreme influencers	Promote intense fitness and exercise often linked to dieting and restricting food intake
'Thinspo' influencers	Promote extremely thin bodies as aspiration and often glorify starvation or unhealthy weight loss
'What I eat in a day' influencers	Share how to restrict your diet in a day and limiting meals or restricting calories
Mukbang influencers	Broadcast themselves eating large amounts of food which can normalise overeating
'Eat like a celebrity' influencers	Promote and mimic eating habits of a celebrity (often thin supermodels)
Weight loss transformation influencers	Promote before and after images through drastic weight loss
Cheat day binge influencers	Promote cheat meals after restricting food or dieting
Extreme calorie counting and speed eating influencers	Promote eating vast numbers of calories or eating large amounts of food quickly in one sitting or in a day
Hyper-sexualised and 'baddie' influencers	Focus on what you look like and its link to sex appeal which often focuses on surgically enhanced body promotion
Beauty ideal influencers	Filtered and edited photos which promote unattainable beauty ideals or cosmetic surgery

Figure 5: Different types of social media influencers and what they promote.

Parents and professionals shared their concerns how children and young people's online use could have a negative impact on a child's body image and appearance. A parent of a 16 year old expressed her concerns about her daughter's use of filter editing and the impact on her mental wellbeing:

> *"My daughter always struggled with how she looked and how others saw her online... I was shocked when I saw her social media profile how she had changed her image with filters... she was completely unrecognisable!"*

Another parent said they were:

> *"very concerned about online content and comparisons that make children feel not good enough or not thin enough".*

A practitioner expressed their concerns about how online use could lead to:

> *"a negative impact on body image, unrealistic ideals and teenage girls who want to achieve the image of people who have been cosmetically altered or use filters – an image which would be difficult to achieve naturally".*

Finally, a teacher shared their concern with the *"constant obsession with selfies perpetuates young people looking and judging themselves as not being adequate enough – not thin or beautiful enough and often for the boys, not muscly or fit enough".*

Practical TIPS: Practical tips on promoting positive body image online and appearance

It is important to celebrate and embrace diversity to promote positive and healthy body image and appearance amongst children and young people. The following practical tips include ideas to help parents, carers and professionals promote positive online body image:

- Encourage your child to review and delete any social media accounts and platforms that they feel have a negative effect on their own body image.
- Try and model positive body image behaviours and language by not body-shaming your child, yourself and others by making negative comments on body shape and appearance both on and offline. It is important to set an example and model healthy and positive body image through the acceptance of your own and other people's body shapes.
- Create space and time to keep having open and honest discussions with your child on self-acceptance, the importance of positive body image and the impact of social media on their own perception of both their own body and other people's bodies.
- Help children and young people recognise how the online appearance of others can be easily distorted and that images do not always reflect real life. It is important to remind them that with the use photo-editing, face-tuning apps and image editing through filters it is easy for images and features to be manipulated.
- If you are concerned about both your child's mental health and a radical change in their diet due to the content that they have seen online, it is important to seek professional support.

Activities to promote positive body image through social media

1. Positive social influencers

Identify different social influencers (beauty, fashion, celebrities and fitness social influencers) and discuss how they portray positive body image. Discuss whether any of the images or content feels 'real' and authentic and which looks like it has been edited, filtered or enhanced. Determine which influencers are good ambassadors for positive body image for other children and young people.

2. Selfie talk

Have an open selfie talk about digital distortion – discuss why and how social influencers, friends and they themselves would want to change and distort an image when taking a selfie?

3. Body positive journal

Encourage your child to create a body positive journal by trying to help them appreciate what their body can do and what they enjoy rather than just how their body looks. Some ideas for prompts include:

- The four things I like most about myself are…
- I am happiest when I am…
- The three things that make me feel most confident are…
- What are some of the amazing things that your body allows you to do that make you feel positive and happy?

For more information, advice and support

The Mental Health Foundation has produced a body image guide for parents and caregivers. https://www.mentalhealth.org.uk/sites/default/files/2022-06/Body-Image-Guide-for-Parents-and-Caregivers.pdf

BEAT provides resources for parents and professionals on eating disorders.
https://www.beateatingdisorders.org.uk/

Internet Matters provides tips to promote body image.
https://www.internetmatters.org/resources/promoting-positive-body-image-with-children/

Young Minds provides tips and advice on how to find professional help for eating disorders. https://www.youngminds.org.uk/young-person/coping-with-life/body-image/

Childline provides counselling, support and information for children and young people.
https://childline.org.uk/

Dove Self-esteem Project – provides body confidence and self-esteem education.
https://www.dove.com/uk/dove-self-esteem-project.html

References

Bell, C. (2024) *Active and Passive Social Media Use: Relationships with body image in physically active men*. Sage Publishing.

Ofcom (2024) *Online Nation Report*, Ofcom.

Internet Matters/BMG (2024) *Children's Wellbeing in a Digital World: Year Three Index Report 2024*. (https://www.internetmatters.org/hub/research/childrens-wellbeing-in-a-digital-world-index-report-2024/).

C – Catfishing

The chapter will cover:

- An overview of what catfishing means.
- Why people catfish and how catfishing operates.
- The warning signs of catfishing.
- What to do if your child has been catfished.
- Parents, carers and professionals' views of catfishing.
- Practical tips and activities on preventing catfishing.

What is catfishing?

Catfishing is a growing online phenomenon amongst both adults and children. Catfishing is a form of online deception and happens when someone uses fake information or a false identity to make you believe that you are in an online relationship with them. Once you are in a 'relationship' with them, a 'catfisher' may threaten to share images or secrets online to friends or family which can cause stress, embarrassment and anxiety. In some cases, catfishers may ask for money or steal personal identities using the information that has been shared with them. Catfishing can occur from individuals based anywhere in the world. Catfishers tend to work through a variety of platforms including social media, dating apps and messaging platforms.

Why do people catfish?

There are potentially many reasons why people engage in catfishing online, from doing it for fun or out of boredom to wanting to exert control or for attention. Of greatest concern are those who engage in catfishing as predators to build trust to sexually groom and exploit children and young people (see O – Online Safety). Janneke Schokkenbroek, in her article '*Behind the Mask: Why Do People Catfish*' (2025), identifies additional reasons why people engage in catfishing, for example, it could include people who are:

- Looking for a connection due to loneliness or not feeling confident about their 'real selves'.
- Escaping their troubles and struggles offline.
- Looking for the thrill of deception or seeing it as a game.
- Looking to pass time and out of curiosity.
- Looking to explore parts of their identity that they are not able to share with the world.
- Looking to gain affection or attention.

How does catfishing operate?

It can be really hard for a young person to determine the authenticity of someone new that they are communicating with online. However, nowadays, with many young people meeting others virtually, it is important to be extremely cautious when embarking on any new online relationship.

Many parents, carers and professionals were interested to know how catfishing operates. Catfishing often happens through some of the following stages, when a catfisher:

- Creates a fake profile (often using photos/personal stories stolen from others).
- Works to gain trust with a victim – often through flattery or promoting shared interests.
- Sends messages to the victim using a fake profile.
- Rarely suggest meeting face to face.
- May exploit their victim through one or more of the following:
  a. financial fraud
  b. emotional fraud

c. relationship fraud
d. identity theft
e. sextortion.

What are the catfishing warning signs?

- Do they ask for personal information e.g. address, information about family members, friends or pets, hobbies etc?
- Do they ask for money including crypto currency, gaming credits or vouchers?
- Do they ask for pictures, videos or photos? Do they ask for intimate photos or videos?
- Do they ask you to keep secrets?
- Do they know a lot about you – your friends, family, hobbies etc?
- Do they tend to not use a camera when they are communicating?
- Do they want to move conversations to other platforms so that they can direct message?

Does it all sound too good to be true? It is important to be proactive and stay aware of potential catfishing risks.

Parents, carers and professionals' views of catfishing

Whilst many parents, carers and professionals noted how social media was a positive way for children and young people to connect and interact with others, the issue of catfishing was recognised as a negative concern and fear. For example, one parent noted that her daughter had been involved:

> *"It was an awful scam. She (daughter) was approached by someone claiming to be a friend of a friend. She was speaking to him every night and was so happy she had met someone. She was devastated when she found out…. feeling betrayed and stupid. It's really affected her confidence… and she doesn't trust people now".*

Another parent said:

> *"The internet is a scary place… I've been catfished myself and it really affected me mentally. I worry about my kids!"*

However, for many, there was a naivete about how catfishing operated and how to help protect children and young people.

Practical TIPS Practical tips on preventing catfishing

There are various ways to protect your child from being catfished. Here are some examples of practical tips for you to share with your child:

- **Talk with your child** about the risks of catfishing online. It is important to talk openly so that your child is not embarrassed to share their concerns about catfishing or report it if they have been involved in catfishing or online deception.
- Encourage your child to update their **privacy settings** by reviewing what personal information they share, who can see their personal information and who and how others can comment on their personal information or contents.
- Encourage your child to **check the name and social media profile** of the person that they are communicating with and who are they friends with. Do they give them lots of compliments? Does it all seem too good to be true?
- Encourage your child to be careful about what **images are posted online** of themselves which could lead to identify fraud or even catfishers targeting based on similar interests. For example, clubs and activities they are involved in or the names of friends etc.
- Tell your child to **BLOCK** anyone they have any concerns about or feel uncomfortable about.

What do to if your child has been catfished

- **Stay calm and listen** to what your child has to say. Try to be non-judgemental and reassure them that they are not to blame – they may feel embarrassed or ashamed.
- If your child has been catfished – stop all conversations with the catfisher, screen shot and **report** fake accounts. **Block them!**
- **Collate evidence** by taking screenshots of any messages and names. Do not delete any information as this information may be needed in evidence.
- **Reassure** your child of the positive impact of letting you know that they have been catfished and encourage them to come to you again, if they are worried or concerned.
- Seek out **additional information and support** if you or your child are a victim of catfishing.
- **Report any incident to the Police.**

For more information and advice on catfishing

NSPCC provides support on how to keep children safe online.
www.nspcc.org.uk/keeping-children-safe/online-safety/

Childline – confidential support for anyone under 19.
www.childline.org.uk

Thinkuknow – Education site by CEOP for age appropriate online safety.
www.thinkuknow.co.uk

Activity: Helpful reminders that you can share with your child to protect them from catfishing

Having open and regular conversations about the opportunities and risks associated with social media is essential. Why not share these helpful reminders on catfishing with your child and identify any other words that you would associate with catfishing?

C Stay **cautious** of people you interact with online and have never met.

A **Ask** for audio call or video call – catfishers will often refuse to use their camera saying that it is broken.

T Speak to a **trusted** adult if you have any concerns about the person you're speaking with online.

F **Find** out more and do your research about the person you're speaking with online.

I **Ignore** requests for inappropriate photos or money.

S **Set** your profiles to private and don't share intimate photos.

H **Halt** communication with anyone you're speaking with online that makes you feel uncomfortable.

References

Schokkenbroek, J.M. (2025) 'Behind the Mask: Why do people catfish? Unpacking the reasons behind fake online profiles', *Psychology Today US*, 13 January.

D – Deep and dark web

The chapter will cover:

- The differences between the surface, deep and dark web.
- Why children use the dark web and how they can access it.
- Parents, carers and professionals' views of the deep and dark web.
- Practical tips on safeguarding about the dangers of the dark web.

The differences between the surface, deep and dark web

The dark web is a digital underworld which, for many of us, is shrouded in mystery and fear. However, there are different elements to the internet. The **surface web** or World Wide Web refers to all web content which is the visible part of the internet. The **deep web** is hidden from public view and cannot be accessed via a search engine and is often protected by passwords which maintains privacy and security. Whereas the **dark web** is hidden and unregulated and can only be accessed through specific software and allows those who use it to communicate anonymously and avoiding surveillance.

The web iceberg image (p.66) outlines the differences between the surface, deep and a dark web, showing that a huge proportion of web content is hidden from public view.

- **World Wide Web** or otherwise known as surface web which includes all web-based content is available to 4% of the population (Odley, 2023).
- The **deep web** which cannot be accessed by search engines and is often protected through passwords or encryptions is used most widely (90%). Examples of deep web content includes academic data bases, legal documents, online banking, institutional intranets, learning management systems, student, parent and staff portals.
- The hidden **dark web** on the other hand, can only be accessed through specific software and can allow those who use it to communicate anonymously as it is unregulated. The dark web is accessed by only 6%.

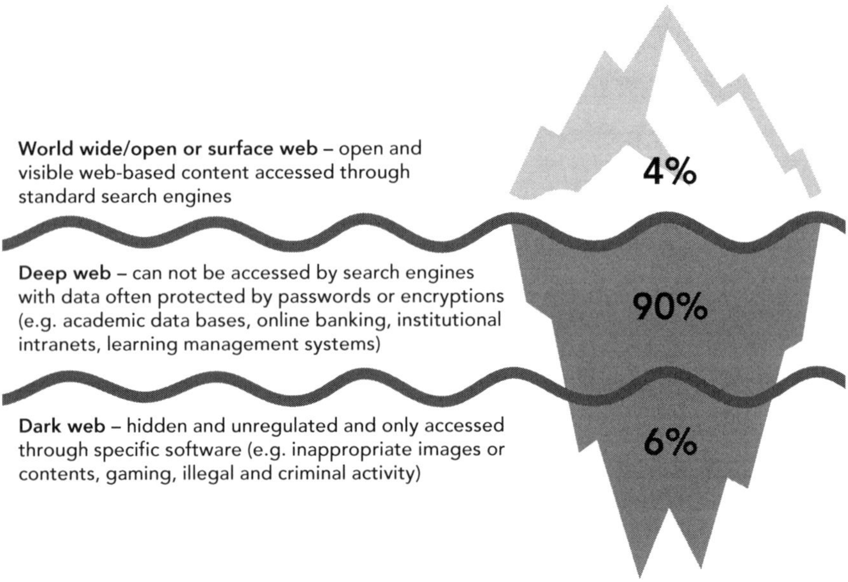

Figure 6: The surface, deep and dark web iceberg

Children and young people and the dark web

Why do they access the dark web?

The dark web is not a safe or appropriate place for children to explore, and it is our responsibility as parents and professionals to safeguard all children and young people against them accessing it. Whilst it is only a small number of children and young people who are able to access the dark web, there are various reasons why they may wish to do so. Some examples are outlined below.

- It is possible to keep and remain anonymous especially for those young people who are worried about being under surveillance or their data being tracked.
- It can be used to share inappropriate and restricted contents and information (e.g. sexual, political, controversial contents). Some young people also may seek information on cybersecurity and hacking through the dark web.
- It can be used for illegal and criminal activity (e.g. trading activity, online grooming, buying and selling drugs or weapons).
- Out of pure interest and curiosity; movies have a tendency to glorify hacking and cyber criminality which can promote curiosity and interest in accessing the dark web.
- To communicate with others anonymously without being tracked.

Whatever the reasons for children and young people accessing the dark web, it can expose them to illegal activities and disturbing content which can potentially have a long-lasting psychological impact.

How do they access the dark web?

The dark web can be accessed through specific software which anonymises the user by directing requests to a central resource and then randomly redirecting the request. In addition, layers of encryption are added which make it difficult to trace the user. This is alternatively known as the 'onion router' (TOR). For any tech-savvy young person to access the dark web, a range of specific knowledge and skills are required – the dark web is not something that you accidentally fall upon online!

What are the risks?

There are a huge range of safeguarding risks to children and young people accessing the surface web as well as the dark web, but the dark web can pose specific risks to children and young people including, for example:

- Being exposed to inappropriate and harmful information, images and content.
- Being exposed to illegal activities (e.g. selling drugs).
- Interacting with online predators which potentially results in child and sexual exploitation.
- Being exposed to radical or extremist images and contents.

Parents, carers and professionals' views of the dark and deep web

Parents were concerned about children's accessing *"illegal and the wrong platforms through the dark web".*

> *"It scares me senseless that they are accessing all this content on the dark web and I wouldn't have a clue what and how they access it, let alone stop it!"*

In addition, professionals noted that:

> *"there is absolutely no reason for kids to seek out the dark web. The best thing to do is talk to teenagers openly about the threats of the dark web."*

Practical TIPS — Practical tips on safeguarding about the dangers of the dark web

As parents and professionals, it is our role to help safeguard children and young people about the dangers of using the dark web. These practical tips will help promote your child's digital safety so that they can safely navigate the online world.

- Make sure you **talk openly** to your child about responsible online activity, how to avoid suspicious websites and the dangers of the dark web (see **O – Online Safety**).
- Encourage age-appropriate regular conversations with your child about digital online safety.
- Encourage them to **talk to trusted adults** if they come across things online that make them feel worried or uncomfortable – they can help provide guidance and support.
- Keep an eye on your child's digital activity by **monitoring** what and how they are accessing digital platforms. Whilst it is important to try and respect your child's privacy, it is also possible to check browsing history.

- Use **parental controls and security software** which can help restrict online activities and help reduce engagement in harmful sites and contents. Check if the onion router (TOR) browser is installed which can indicate that a young person is potentially accessing the dark web. Virtual private networks (VPN) can be used to provide additional security to your child's online activity.
- Use **browser history** to see if anything of concern (browser history can be deleted and children and young people can use private windows or browse in incognito mode). Bear in mind, many tech-savvy young people know how to hide their browsing history.
- **Crypto currency** is often the preferred way through the dark web to make purchases and engage in financial transactions through the dark web. Look out for unexplained transactions and use of crypto currencies.
- If you or your child see anything online that worries you **report it to the Child Exploitation and Online Protection (CEOP)**.

For more information and advice

Children's Society

https://www.childrenssociety.org.uk/sites/default/files/2020-12/What-Is-The-Dark-Web.pdf

Internet Matters

https://www.internetmatters.org/hub/guidance/what-is-the-dark-web-advice-for-parents/

CEOP Education Website for strategies to help your child stay safe online

https://www.ceopeducation.co.uk/

References

Odley, J. (2023) 'What is the deep web?' Acer Corner.

E – Excessive digital use

The chapter will cover:

- An overview of research on excessive digital use.
- Signs of excessive screentime.
- Effects of excessive digital use.
- Views of parents, carers and professionals on excessive digital use.
- Practical tips and activities to promote a balanced approach to online use including family digital agreements, classroom digital agreements and screentime tracker.

How much is too much?

Are you worried that your child is spending too long on their screens? Are they glued to their screens and spending an excessive amount of time online? There is a lot of debate about what 'excessive digital use' is. Some define excessive use of digital media as being like an addiction with children and young people devoting so much time online which ultimately affects the way they live their lives, their physical health and their mental wellbeing.

What the research tells us

Not only do more children have access to smartphones and digital devices, but the use of social media is also growing rapidly amongst children.

Figures for the UK show that:

- By the age of eleven, 91% of children own a smartphone (Ofcom, 2024).
- A quarter of 5- to 7-year-olds own a smartphone.
- Three quarters (76%) use a tablet (Ofcom, 2024).
- Ofcom (February 2024) states that three-quarters of social media users between the age of 8 and 17 have their own account or profile on at least one of the large social media platforms.
- What's more, most social media platforms have a minimum age of 13, but six in every ten children aged between 8 and 12 years old have signed up with their own account.
- As a nation, we spend more and more time online. *Ofcom's Media Lives Report* (2024) states that many children in the UK spend between six and eight hours a day online.

Despite spending more time online, children and young people – as well as adults – appear to be concerned about their screentime. The *Children's Media Literacy Report* (Ofcom 2024) identified that over a third (35%) of 8- to 17-year-olds feel that their own screentime is too high. It found that older children are more likely to be aware of their own excessive online use: 44% of 16- to 17-year-olds agree that their screentime is too high compared to 31% of 8 to11 year olds.

What are some of the signs of too much screen time?

Are you worried your child is spending too much time or even too dependent on their screens?

Is your child:

- Finding it difficult to concentrate and easily distracted?
- Prefer to use their screens rather than being involved in an alternative fun activity?
- Have a meltdown if you take their screen away?
- Have problems sleeping due to using their screens late at night?
- Prefer to use their screens rather than be out with friends?

One of the main reasons that children and young people participate in excessive online use is algorithms. Algorithms are tools used by technology companies which watch our online behaviour and determine what we are accessing digitally. Many algorithms are not only based on our interests and what information we are accessing but also on what other people our predicted age are interested in. They exist to channel content on our perceived interests which ultimately encourages more time spent on screen! If you play specific games online, comment, like or share specific content, technology companies through algorithms will note that you enjoyed it and offer you more of the same type of content.

However, algorithms can also result in being sent negative content which affects children and young people's online safety and their mental health. If a child has inadvertently or purposefully shared or liked negative contents, an algorithm will pick this up and share further negative and similar contents (see O – Online Safety). One practitioner, realising the importance of the impact of algorithms on children's online usage, stated:

> *"Encourage them to engage with positive content – tech works from algorithms, so the more funny dog videos they like, the more funny videos will show up! In the same way, the more upsetting and distressing content we engage with, the more shows up".*

What are the potential effects of excessive digital use?

Although we have seen that the use of digital technology can have a number of benefits, the potential effects of excessive digital use or digital overload can include, for example:

- **Disturbed and disrupted sleep** – A poor night's sleep can affect a child's mood, often making it difficult for them to function during the day and learn in the classroom due to feelings of tiredness. Technology use has been a big topic of debate with regards to sleep; there are those who argue that the blue light on a screen can have an impact on an individual's sleep by hampering with melatonin, the hormone which is responsible for your sleep cycle. There are others (Bauducco, 2024) that say it does not have as much of an effect as we first thought and instead recognise that technology before sleep may also be time consuming, help regulate emotions whilst trying to fall asleep and/or to help facilitate sleep itself (e.g. listening to music, or listening to podcasts and sleep or meditation apps).

- **Weight gain or obesity** – Children who overuse digital media tend to be less likely to be physically active which can lead to weight gain. The World Health Organisation (WHO) has issued guidelines emphasising the importance of reducing screentime in young children as a measure to prevent childhood obesity (WHO, 2019). It is important to try and encourage a healthy balance of screen time and physical activity.
- **Digital eye strain** – Excessive digital use can lead to digital eye strain which can lead to dry eyes. blurred vision and even headaches. Research (Coles-Brennan, 2021) has suggested that as many as 90% of users of digital devices experience 'digital eye strain' which is characterised by stresses on the ocular environment.
- **Social interaction with others** – Too much screen time can limit your child's social interactions with friends and family. This potentially could impact on their ability to gain social skills and build relationships with others. One clinician consulted with, noted that:

> *"the addiction to online platforms is so concerning… the way it impacts their socialising skills and overall mental health as a result is something we (clinicians) are becoming more and more aware of".*

Views of parents, carers and professionals on excessive digital use

Parents, carers and professionals are concerned about digital overload and the impact of chidlren's excessive digital use on their wellbeing. Parents shared that they were:

> *"really concerned, my child stays in their bedroom all day online and rarely does anything else";*

> *"being online is like an addiction for him (my 15 year old child) – he is obsessed";*

"I am really concerned, he spends every waking moment on his phone, scrolling mindlessly, but what can I do?"

The comments from professionals included:

"The amount of time spent on these platforms is alarming and I can see definite links between this and impact on their mental health".

"The amount of time spent on devices is causing a severe impact on communication, interacting with peers and desensitization to the real world".

Parents and professionals offered a wealth of practical tips on how to reduce excessive digital use and many of which are embedded within this Guide. They include, for example, setting boundaries, seeking offline alternatives, restricting use, banning phones at home and school, using innovative technology to support mental health and wellbeing, modelling behaviour and, most importantly, the need for continuous open and non-judgemental conversations.

Practical TIPS – Practical tips on promoting healthy digital activity and avoiding excessive use

There are a number of ways that you can help your child reduce their excessive and addictive digital use. Some of practical tips include:

- **Try not to remove access to digital platforms or social media as a punishment** as often children and young people may be inclined to use technology secretively and in isolation.
- Try and encourage **regular open conversations** about their digital use and the implications of excessive and addictive use. Try not to have these discussions in the heat of the moment or during an argument about online use!

- Encourage your child to **limit their screentime before bed**. For example, by coming off their phones at least 30 – 60 minutes before they go to bed and putting 'do not disturb' notifications on. If your child's phone works as an alarm in the morning, invest in an alarm clock!
- Encourage your child to take **screen breaks**. Why not follow the 20:20:20 rule – look away from your screens every 20 mins and look at something at least 20 feet away for 20 seconds at least!
- Encourage your child to register with online services using their **real age** to help prevent them accessing content that is suitable for people who are older.
- If possible, encourage your child to **self-regulate their usage** of technology through open conversations by helping them set their own boundaries about healthy digital use. For example, agreeing clear boundaries for where and when screens can be used. Try leaving phones in another room charging at bedtimes, agree no phones at the dinner table.
- Why not **track how much time** you and your children are spending on screens every day? Set you and your family goals to reduce the time spent on screens. There are various technology tools to control screen use. Many tech manufacturers allow you to identify screen access data and set content and time limits on digital use.
- Take an online break – organise a **family digital detox or digital break** to help the whole family disconnect from their screens. Encourage activities that don't rely on digital media but promote physical activity instead.
- Reset what your child sees online by **clearing algorithms**. Some apps have settings which can delete your algorithm and help retrain the digital application to show a different style of content.

Activities to promote healthy digital consumption and avoid excessive screentime

Two activities have been developed for you to complete with children and young people to help promote healthy digital use:

1. Family digital agreement
2. Classroom digital agreement

1. Creating a family digital agreement

What is a family digital agreement?

A family digital agreement can provide children with a clear digital routine and advocates both a positive and meaningful use of technology. A whole family digital approach also promotes healthy online habits by setting boundaries for the use of digital technology within the family both in and out of the home.

A family digital agreement can help provide consistency so that everyone in the family knows the rules of technology use. It can also promote online safety and responsible and healthy digital usage. What is more, it tends to prevent conflict and arguments about digital use because the agreement can define ground rules, limits and expectations within the family's use of technology.

You could start by discussing the benefits and barriers of the use of digital technology including smartphones, tablets, computers, TVs and gaming devices. All members of the family should be encouraged to work together to co-design a shared family digital agreement. Whilst there are many family technology agreements online, this agreement could be drawn or designed by all members of the family which personalises it and ensures that it is jointly owned by everyone.

How to create a family digital agreement

No family is the same and as a result every family digital agreement will be different. Plan and co-design the family agreement together and when things are calm at home, not just after an argument over your child's use of technology! We encourage you to keep it simple and ensure that it also includes parents' and even grandparents' digital use too! Children are also encouraged to be creative and help with its design and production.

> **Helpful hint:** It is really important to encourage everyone in the family to sign up to the agreement and it is visible around the home. Why not put copies in different parts of the house – on the fridge in the kitchen and in bedrooms?

Whilst all family digital agreements will be different, a family digital plan could include:

- **Screentime limits** (e.g. no phones at bedtimes or during mealtimes).

- **Knowledge of age limits** and keeping to these as a family – helps ensure younger siblings are not viewing content that is meant for older children.
- **Digital usage and appropriate content** (e.g. age-appropriate restrictions and a good balance of screentime and spending time offline).
- **Digital netiquette** (e.g. showing kindness and respect to others online).
- **Digital safety and security** (e.g. keeping devices secure through password use, asking permission before sharing information and asking for help if children see or hear something online that makes them worried or sad and agreeing which apps or websites are off limits).
- **Consequences and rewards** (e.g. family compliance to the digital agreement could lead to treats, offers of spending more time together as a family, or positive words of encouragement, whilst breaking digital agreement could lead to the loss of screentime).
- **Looking after digital devices and keeping them safe** – inside and outside the home.

Family digital plans can be designed with and for children of all ages. It is important to set realistic expectations so that rules that are created and agreed are age-specific. We suggest that families keep talking about their digital use and revisit the plans collectively as a family to ensure it still serves a purpose, and update it when it is needed, especially when new platforms or technology are available and used.

When should I create a family digital agreement?

It is never too early to create a family digital agreement together. Children as young as 3 years old can contribute to a family digital plan to help understand healthy digital habits. Young children may be accessing different technology and may need more structure, different types of rules and consequences. If you create your own family digital plan with children under the age of 5, use pictures and photos to make it bright and seen by all the family. For those families with primary school age children, creating a family culture for screentime is essential whether at school or at home. Again, these can be creatively discussed and designed by all the family. A parent of younger children said:

"We put a sticker chart next to our family digital agreement .... we reinforce positive behaviour.... by having a family treat at the end of the week if we got 6 stickers".

Another parent of a girl aged 12 said:

"We drew a Jones Family Digital Plan and put it on the fridge. Even the grandparents help put it together and we coloured in the pictures together. Granny also took a copy and put it on her own fridge. We all enjoyed making it!"

As your children grow older, it is important to adapt family digital plans; discussing and co-designing a family digital plan with your teenagers is helpful. You may be surprised at what digital limits and suggestions teenagers may have.

Helpful hint: Parents should try and lead by example with responsible digital behaviour. Children often mimic their parents' behaviour and learn from watching how their parents interact with technology. If parents don't follow the family digital agreement rules, the agreement is hard to enforce.

Whilst we encourage you to create your own personalised Family Digital Agreement, there are many examples of agreements online. We have created an example of a family digital plan that can be customised by you and your family (see p.80).

The ______ Family Digital Agreement

This is the ______ Family Digital Agreement, and I will follow these family digital rules and I will:-

Family Screentime

- make sure that I am aware of how much time I am spending on screen and only use my devices for
  ______ (hours) ______ (mins) during weekdays
  ______ (hours) ______ (mins) during the weekend and holidays
- make sure that I have a good balance between spending time on screens and spending time offline and will spend at least ______ (hours) and ______ (minutes) each day doing things that do not require a screen
- make sure that all my devices are turned off at ______ (time) during weekdays and ______ (time) at weekends

Family Screen Free Zones

- respect that we have family screen free zones in the house which includes ______
  (e.g. mealtimes, the car, garden, bedrooms etc)

Family Screen Safety

- ask permission before I download any apps or games or buy anything online
- only chat with people I know, including family and friends especially when using social media or gaming
- will not share any personal information or passwords online
- if I see or hear anything online that makes me feel worried, upset or scared I will ask for help. I know that I will not be in trouble for sharing my worries with a trusted adult as they will help me deal with my online concerns

Family Netiquette

- show kindness and respect when communicating with others online
- look after all my devices and other people's devices both inside and outside the house

Any other digital wellbeing rules that are best for our family

______

______

We will talk about the family digital agreement and check that it is working every ______ (days/months)

Family Signatures

Name ______ Signature ______ Name ______ Signature ______

Name ______ Signature ______ Name ______ Signature ______

Name ______ Signature ______ Name ______ Signature ______

Date: ______

This resource is available to download at:

https://pavpub.com/mental-health/a-to-z-guide-to-children-and-young-peoples-digital-mental-health-resources

2. School and college digital agreement

In a similar way to family digital agreements, a school or college digital agreement can be co-created with teachers, parents, school governors and, most importantly, pupils or students. Co-produced rules on digital use at school or college is important because it can help minimise pupils being distracted by their screens, encourages pupils to use technology responsibly and safely and encourages social interaction within the classroom. A set of clear rules can ultimately encourage positive school digital citizenship and help maintain a positive learning and teaching environment for both pupils and teaching staff. We have created an example of a school and college digital agreement and a set of rules that can be customised and adapted according to the age of pupils. Like the family digital plan, it is important to review the plan with pupils and parents regularly (see below).

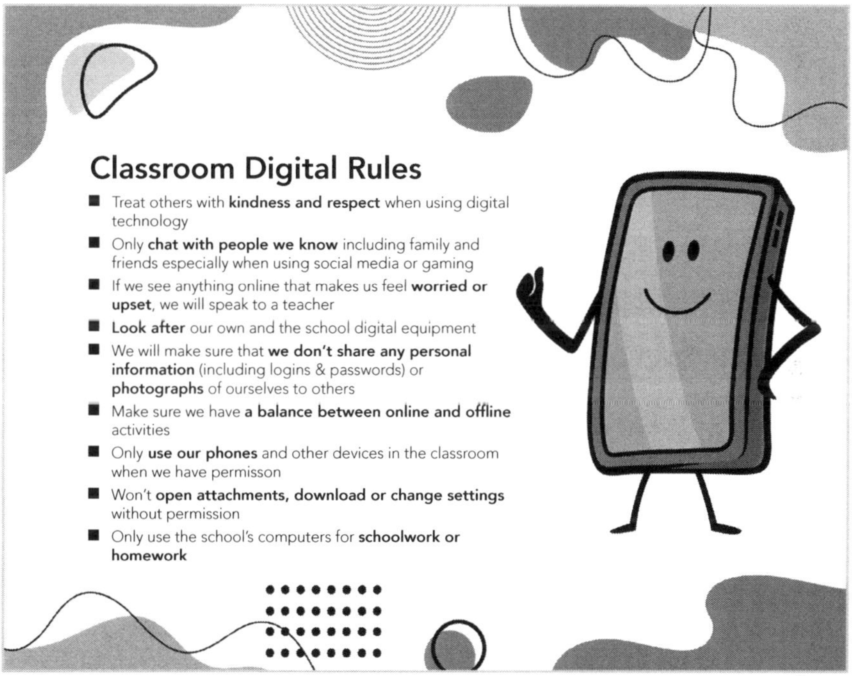

For more information and support

Example of downloadable family digital plans

Internet Matters have downloadable family digital plans that can be adapted ://www.internetmatters.org/resources/digital-family-agreement-template/

References

Bauducco, S. *et al* (2024) A bidirectional model of sleep and technology use: A theoretical review of how much, for whom, and which mechanisms, *Sleep Medicines Review,* 76, August.

Ofcom (2024) 'A window into young children's online worlds'. Ofcom.

Coles-brennan, C., Sulley, A. & Young, G. (2019) Management of digital eye strain. *Clinical and Experimental Optometry, 102* (1), 18–29. https://doi.org/10.1111/cxo.12798

Ofcom (2024) *Children's Media Literacy Report*. Ofcom.

Ofcom (2022) *Children and Parents' Media Use and Attitudes Report*. Ofcom. https://www.ofcom.org.uk/media-use-and-attitudes/media-habits-children/children-and-parents-media-use-and-attitudes-report-2022

https://www.ofcom.org.uk/online-safety/protecting-children/how-the-online-safety-act-will-help-to-protect-children (6 February 2024, Ofcom)

Ofcom (2024) *Online Nation*. Ofcom. https://www.ofcom.org.uk/siteassets/resources/documents/research-and-data/online-research/online-nation/2024/online-nation-2024-report.pdf?v=386238

World Health Organization (WHO) (2019) *Guidelines on physical activity, sedentary behaviour and sleep for children under 5 years of age.* World Health Organization.

https://iris.who.int/handle/10665/311664. License: CC BY-NC-SA 3.0 IGO

F – Fake news

The chapter will cover:

- Research on children and young people's access to real and fake news.
- Potential reasons for creating fake news.
- How to identify fake news.
- Views of parents, carers and professionals on fake news.
- Practical tips and activities on tackling fake news.

Definitions and impact

We are constantly being bombarded by news and information through social media platforms and for many of us it is really hard to filter through it to determine what is real and what is not. Fake news is a growing global phenomenon and refers to news that includes false or misleading information which is spread online. Fake news through social media can include news stories, adverts or photo images. It can have a huge impact on children and young people's mental health including triggering trauma and or causing anxiety and low mood. It can reinforce hate speech (see H – Online hate) by promoting racism, extremism and misogyny. It can also cause confusion and mistrust with children and young people not knowing what to believe and not believe.

Fake news that is spread online can be categorised as misinformation and disinformation. On their website, NSPCC define misinformation as being 'false information shared by accident without the intent to cause harm.

For example, sharing inaccurate photos, quotes or dates online'. Therefore, misinformation is often spread unintentionally without the person who is spreading it, realising that what they are spreading is false or wrong. NSPCC defines disinformation as being:

> *'false information shared deliberately to mislead or cause harm. For example, fabricated news stories and political propaganda'.*

Research on children and young people's access to real news and fake news

Ofcom's News Consumption Survey (2023) found that the majority of young people (83% of 16- to 24-year-olds) view news online; 71% of these young people access it through social media. This research found that 12- to 15-year-olds predominantly used Tik Tok (28%), You Tube (25%) and Instagram (25%) to access the news. For these children, their main interests were in celebrity or music-focused news. Despite this, children and young people were fairly reluctant to trust the news they were presented with online. Only a third of 12- to 15-year-olds who accessed news online said that news on social media sites was 'always' or 'mostly true'.

Ofcom (2023) found that nine out of ten 12- to 17-year-olds 'consider' whether they can trust the information they are presented with online. However, few children and young people used rigorous checks to confirm the accuracy of information they were presented with online. For example, 33% children said they checked information across other websites and 24% said they use fact-checking websites.

Ofcom (2024) explored whether children were able to determine what is real and what is fake online. They found that seven out of ten (69%) 12- to 17-year-olds felt confident to assess the difference between real and fake news, in comparison with 67% of 16- to 17-year-olds. Meanwhile, seven out of ten parents expressed their concern that their child would be able to distinguish between real and fake online (Ofcom, 2025).

For young people aged between 12 and 15 years old, TikTok continues to be identified as the most-used single source for news. When looking at specific sources for news, 30% of 12- to 15-year-old news consumers look to TikTok, followed by YouTube (27%) and then Facebook and Instagram (both 21%). However, **their most trustworthy source for news is family**; 78% said that news sourced from their family was always, or mostly, reported truthfully, compared to just over a third (36%) who said the same about news on social media sites or apps (Ofcom, 2025).

Potential reasons for creating fake news

Figure 7: Reasons for creating fake news

There are many reasons that people create fake news which can include:

- Wanting to change people's opinions or views.
- To advertise a product or brand.
- For fun, as a joke or through boredom.
- To gain fame and attention.
- To make money by deceiving people into giving money or through clickbait and advertisement revenue.
- To damage a person's or organisation's reputation through defamation and smearing.
- To create propaganda which can result in political manipulation.

How to identify fake news

Fake news can spread widely and rapidly especially through social media platforms. It is important to have open and honest conversations with your child about how to identify real and fake news and the impact that it has on them and others. Try and help them focus on their critical thinking skills to assess what is real and what is not real.

There are a number of ways for you and your child to spot fake news. For example:

- Be sceptical of social media news – check the facts from other reputable sources (e.g. look to see if other platforms are presenting the same information).
- Run a news story through a fact-checking website.
- Check for poor grammar and spelling – professional articles are less likely to include a number of typos or poorly worded articles.
- Check web addresses as fake websites will be similar to real ones but slightly adapted or misspelt so it's important to check URLs.
- Research the organisation who is publishing the information. Does it look credible and genuine?

Parents, carers and professionals' views of fake news

Parents articulated their concerns about their children being able to determine the difference between real and fake news online. One parent stated that:

> *"it is so difficult for anyone, especially children and young people, to decide what is the truth and what are the lies on social media… what is fact and what is fiction".*

Another parent said:

> *"It's amazing that children feel that they are up to date with all the world news from viewing YouTube and memes. They don't seem to question the authenticity of what they see and hear through social media."*

A teacher fed back that:

> *"It is so worrying how much children believe... It is the hoaxes and lies....it can be so disturbing for children as they don't know what is real and what is fake".*

Practical TIPS Practical tips on tackling fake news

To help children and young people navigate the overwhelming flow of information online, here are some practical tips on how to support them:

- Try and encourage children to stop and think whether the information they are reading and hearing is authentic. Promote the importance of critical thinking and encourage them to **think before they comment, share or like information** on news that is presented to them
- Have an **open and honest discussion** with them about the different types of news and information portrayed through social media and why they think some people create fake news stories and the impact that it may have
- Discuss how algorithms can create **echo-chambers**, where they will only see the content that matches their existing beliefs or viewpoints and opposing views can be filtered out. This limits people's perceptions and can reinforce misinformation or biased views
- Discuss with them the **different ways to identify fake news** by checking facts and websites (as outlined above) to help verify fact from fiction

For more information on fake news

Internet Matters provides a guide for parents and interactive quizzes for children and young people https://www.internetmatters.org/issues/fake-news-and-misinformation-advice-hub/

ChildNet provides information and advice on fake news https://www.childnet.com/help-and-advice/fake-news-11-18-year-olds/

NSPCC provides information on the risks and how to spot hoaxes and misinformation https://www.nspcc.org.uk/keeping-children-safe/online-safety/inappropriate-explicit-content/fake-news/

References

Ofcom (2023) *News Consumption in the UK:2023 – Research Findings*. Ofcom.

Ofcom (2023) *Understanding Online Communications Among Children – Quantitative Research*. Ofcom.

Ofcom (2024) *Children and Parents: Media Use and Attitudes Report*. Ofcom.

Ofcom (2025) *Children and Parents: Media Use and Attitudes Report*. Ofcom.

G – Gaming

The chapter will cover:

- An overview of research on children and young people's online gaming activity.
- Examples of different types of online games.
- Reasons why children and young people enjoy gaming, and the risks involved.
- Views of parents, carers, professionals and young people.
- Practical tips and activities to help parents and professionals promote positive online gaming activity

The virtual world

Gaming is hugely popular with children and young people using a range of devices and platforms including social media, computers, consoles or smartphones. Online gaming is a multi-billion pound global industry and allows people to connect all over the world. Although gaming in a virtual world for many children and young people is fun, providing the ability to connect with others and sparking an element of creativity, there are several risks associated to online gaming identified by parents and professionals, including addiction and online safety.

Research on online gaming

Ofcom has identified an increase in children who are gaming online in its *Children and Parents: Media Use and Attitudes Report* (Ofcom, 2024). This report states that:

- The number of children aged between 3 and 17 years old gaming online rose from 57% in 2022 to 60% in 2024.

It found that children use gaming **to communicate with their friends:**

- Nearly a third (31%) of children aged 8 to 17 years old who game online, chat whilst gaming with people they do not know.
- By comparison, two thirds (64%) of children chat to friends or those they know through gaming.

Children and young people are using a range of gaming devices from smartphones and consoles to interactive virtual reality (VR) or augmented reality (AR). Ofcom identified that 5–11 year olds are more likely to use tablets for gaming, whilst mobile phones are used by 59% of 12–15 yearolds. Over 60% of parents say their 8–17 year olds are more likely to use consoles to game.

Gaming is a huge part of children and young people's online culture. Through research to understand online communications (Ofcom 2023) nearly 90% of 11–18 year olds reported gaming at least weekly on one or more platforms; mobile and tablets were the most popular (79%) devices used for gaming.

There are different types of games online which appeal to different audiences and age groups. The *Children and Parents: Media and Attitudes Report* (Ofcom, 2024) found that 45% of 3–17 year olds prefer to play creative and building games, whereas 16–17 year olds prefer to play multi-player games or first-person shooting games.

Types of online games

There are a range of different types of games online which are played on different devices and platforms, some of which include:

- **Mind and puzzle games** – games designed to exercise cognitive abilities including memory and problem solving. These can often be logic based or trivia types of games.

- **Building and creative games** are designed to boost creativity and problem-solving when building and designing.
- **Online casino games** – games that you would play in a casino but are played online.
- **Multi-player games role playing games (PvP)** – games where players compete with other players often as real-time strategy games. These games can include hundreds of players.
- **Realtime shooter games** – shooting combat games played in real time which can be plated in the first person (you see through the character's eyes) or third person where the camera is positioned behind the character playing.
- **Player versus environment (PvE)** – games where players compete against AI instead of other players.
- **Co-operative gameplay** – usually between 2–4 players with only those who have been invited.
- **First person shooting games (FPS)** – player playing in the first person in games that are often combative action games.

Why do children and young people like gaming?

Figure 8: Reasons for gaming online

There are many positive reasons that children and young people like gaming which include:

- For fun and to relax and destress!
- For reward and accomplishment.

- As a time filler.
- Chance to demonstrate skills including problem-solving and creativity.
- Chance to compete with the game itself or friends.
- Meet, interact, connect and socialise with friends. Young people can connect over their shared interest in a game and in some games, join together and work as a team.
- Being autonomous – the chance to be in charge of a character, what it looks like and what games to play.
- A way to escape from the real world.

Risks

Whilst there are lots of positives, there are also risks to gaming. Potential risks include:

- **Online bullying** which could include unkind messages or hate speech.
- **Spending too much money online** – in-game purchases provide a gamer with additional features, weapons, lives or levels. These purchases can be through in-game currency, but this is linked to real cash which can result in spending too much money or even debt. Many even see gaming as a form of gambling (see Gambling).
- **Potential access to inappropriate content** – age rating of games is regulated by PEGI in the UK which sets clear boundaries of how old a child needs to be to buy a game. Games can feature a wide range of content including violence, sex and horror. PEGI uses ratings and content descriptors to give parents and educators information to help parents and educators decide which games are suitable for their children to play.
- **Violent video games** can include 'shooter' or roleplaying games which potentially can encourage aggressive, violent and hostile behaviours and language.
- Potential access to **harmful relationships** if children or young people are 'chatting' with others. Many multi-player games have online chat facilities which allow them to converse with fellow players which could increase their exposure to cyberbullying and online grooming.

Parents, carers and professionals' views of gaming

Parents and professionals thought that gaming was a positive way of children and young people communicating and connecting with their friends and peers. However, many also shared their concerns of the time spent gaming and issues around online safety whilst playing with others, especially those their children did not know. They were also concerned about the effect it has on children's mental health especially their mood and behaviour.

Some teachers expressed their concerns about gaming on their pupil's mental health. One teacher noted that:

> *"Whilst I know it is how kids connect online, my concerns lie with the time they spend online gaming – it's just a time filler! I am concerned with the number of students that come in exhausted because they have been up all-night gaming and then it's impossible for them to learn because they are too tired".*

Several parents commented on how gaming affected the mood and behaviour of their children. One parent of a 16 year old boy shared that:

> *"The problem is I never really know what's going on behind his bedroom door, who he is speaking to or what he is playing. It definitely affects his mood, depending on how long he has been on his games".*

Another parent noted that:

> *"It's the violent games – I just hear him shouting and screaming at the computer. I thought games were supposed to be fun. He just seems to get angry and competitive. It affects his mood ….. he just gets so angry so easily".*

Many parents commented on their concerns about the time children and young people spent gaming online.

> *"It used to drive me mad that my son (aged 14) would never respond when dinner was on the table, couldn't hear me because he had his gaming headphones in. We used to argue. He got cross with me because the games are programmed that if you leave a game without it finishing; the others you are in the game with are penalised as the game automatically stops. He didn't want to let his friends down. When I realised this, I tried to set 10 minute warnings of when dinner was ready."*

Another parent mentioned that:

> *"trying to prize my child away from a game to do everyday activities is so difficult..... he would spend 24 hours a day gaming if he could."*

The positive impact of gaming was also noted by parents and professionals, for example, a social worker stated that:

> *"connecting with others through gaming is a positive way to maintain friendships and stop them feeling lonely..... lots of young people I work with report that gaming can be relaxing and help them manage their mood".*

Another professional noted that:

> *"It is the gaming community that has brought friendships to my patient and stopped her feeling so isolated".*

A clinician shared that he used:

> *"online therapeutic games as an additional therapy tool to support my patient's path to recovery".*

What did young people say about online gaming?

We heard about the importance and impact of gaming from young people. One young person said

> *"For 2 years during Covid (when I was 16) I played video games and Playstation for up to 8 hours a day. It was a way to escape issues from real life……withdraw from 'life'. I played with my friends and cousin, and it was helpful as there was always someone to play with….looking back it feels like I was wasting my life. I could have been doing other things like playing football."*

Another young person said that she and her boyfriend have been gaming for years since she was a teenager. She enjoys gaming because it brings her together with her friends and gives her new experiences and adventures. She reflected that when she immerses herself in a game, she plays out a story that she would never play out in real life. She enjoys games that are lifelike but prefers more fantasy games, playing on her own or multi-player. Gaming provides her with a sense of community and a place to hang out with friends, join group chats, play games and stay up until the early hours of the morning. She notes that often a call is constantly open so there will be always someone on the call to play with…. all day every day. She talked about the cost of games and equipment being a negative aspect of gaming and acknowledged that whilst you can meet "*mean and nasty people*" online, you can also create lifelong online relationships.

Practical TIPS Practical tips on promoting positive online gaming activity

- Gaming for a lot of children is fun, a good way to "chill" and meet friends. Having **open conversations** with your child and **showing an interest in the games your child plays**. Ask your child what they and their friends enjoy about gaming and why. Discuss what they feel happens to them if they play for a long time. **Ask for demonstrations on how the game is played or play the game with them** and familiarise yourself with the games they are playing.
- Encourage your child to play online games for **fun** and not purely to disconnect from the real world or as a stress reliever.
- Encourage your child to only **communicate with people that they know and to never share personal information** or photos (see O – Online Safety).
- Try to keep gaming systems **out of the bedroom** which allows you to monitor or be aware of what, how and how often games are being played.
- Discuss with your child how much **money is and can be spent** on in-game purchases. Turn off or restrict in-game purchases through mobile or console app stores.
- Encourage your child to **be aware of who they are "chatting"** with online whilst gaming. Many multi-player games have online chat facilities which allow them to converse with fellow players to reduce their exposure to cyberbullying, online grooming or any other inappropriate activity.
- Set **clear boundaries** by encouraging your child to limit the time they spend gaming online to be certain times of the day for certain periods of time. Monitor the time spent gaming online – encourage your child to set timers as a reminder to engage in alternative activities or take a break from gaming.

Activity – Gaming lingo quiz

Do you feel out the loop with the language that children and young people use whilst gaming?   Feel out of your depth with the gaming slang? Children and young people use a range of language and slang whilst gaming, often to help them communicate quickly, for some secretly with those they are playing and others who want to look cool. For parents and professionals, it is difficult to understand or keep up to date with some of the gaming terms that children and young people use.

How many of these gaming words are you aware of and what do they mean?

agro	smurf	Newb	AFK	BM	GG	Hacks
griefing	owned	trash	BRB	KYS	Gtg/g2g	Troll
PVP	PVE	PVPVE	FPS	DLC	XP	Cheese

Children and young people will have different meanings for different gaming words, these are some of the potential definitions:

Agro	Aggressive play
Smurf	Underestimated player
Newb	New or inexperienced player
AFK	Away from keyboard
BM	Bad manners or said if a player is being rude or insulting other players
GG	Great game
Hacks	Used at the end of a game if a player loses it is an excuse for losing
Griefing	Hassling or harassing other players online and on purpose
Owned	Describes a player who is badly or easily beaten in game

Trash	Someone is back at the game
BRB	Be right back
KYS	Kill yourself
gtg/g2g	Got to go
Troll	A player who tries to disrupt a game or annoy others. Often, they sabbotage their own teams play
PVP	Player versus player
PVE	Player versus environment ie player fighting computer-controlled enemies
PVPVE	Player versus player versus environment ie fighting players as well as computer-controlled enemies
FPS	First person shooter
DLC	Downloadable content
XP	Experience points. Many games use a levelling system and the more points earned, the more things they can unlock.
Cheese	Tactic in game that may be considered cheap, unfair or easy, which does not require skill to complete a task

For further information and support for parents, carers and professionals on gaming

There are a number of organisations that offer support for children, their parents, carers and professionals and those working with them on online gaming.

Ygam (Young Gamers and Gamblers Education Trust) – provides resources and support for young people struggling with gaming and gambling. www.ygam.org

Internet Matters Online gaming advice hub
https://www.internetmatters.org/advice/by-activity/online-gaming-advice-hub

Young Minds offers information to help parents create a positive culture around gaming and advice if your child's mental health is affected by gaming https://www.youngminds.org.uk/parent/parents-a-z-mental-health-guide/gaming/

Child Exploitation and Online Protection Command (CEOP) provides information and advice for parents and carers on gaming – https://www.ceopeducation.co.uk/parents/articles/gaming/

References

Ofcom (2024) *Children and Parents: Media Use and Attitudes Report*. Ofcom.

Ofcom (2023) *Understanding Online Communications Among Children – Quantitative Research*. Ofcom.

H – Online hate

The chapter will cover:

- An overview of research on online hate.
- Different types and characteristics of online hate.
- The impact of online hate.
- Views of parents, carers and professionals.
- Practical tips on supporting your child to tackle and prevent online hate.

Online hate/cyberhate/hate speech

Are you concerned about how online hate might affect children and young people and its potential impact on their mental wellbeing? Online hate or otherwise known as 'cyberhate' involves posting or sharing hateful contents including abusive or threatening and derogatory language (hate speech) about other people online. This can ultimately encourage discrimination, violence or hatred based on an individual's gender identity, race, religion and beliefs, sexual orientation or disability.

Research on online hate

Internet Matters (2024) found that children and young people were reporting that they are being exposed to online harm with over two thirds of children noting that they had experienced online harm which included:

- 21% being contacted by a stranger.
- 17% being exposed to hate speech.
- 16% being bullied online.

Through their research they found that the majority of parents (92%) were becoming more concerned about at least one online harm. Parents' concerns about the instances and types of harms their children might see increased by nearly a quarter for radical and extremist content, and by 15% for hate speech.

Research suggests that there continues to be a gender imbalance between those who experience hurtful online interactions, as girls are more likely than boys to be subjected to nasty online interactions. Ofcom (2025) found that 34% of girls said that they had experienced this in comparison with 28% of boys. (See M – Misogyny.)

In the UK, two-thirds of teenagers and young adults have encountered at least one potentially harmful piece of content online. However, only one in six of these go on to report it (Ofcom, 2023) and two-thirds (65%) believe that the benefits of being online outweigh the risks it presents. Finding out the reasons for the low reporting rate, Ofcom found that the main reasons were that 29% didn't see the need to do anything and 12% said they did not know what to do or where to go to report it.

Different types of online hate

Online hate, harassment and threats of violence are a threat to human rights, infringing on rights to privacy, not to be discriminated against and to be free from all violence. Technology can be used to spread hate, misogyny, racism, homophobia and transphobia with damaging effects on those who witness or are a victim of it. Some of the different types of online hate include, for example:

- **Misogyny** is a form of hate which targets women and girls. Online, it can be spread across digital platforms and social media. Misogyny can include various ways of expressing hate towards women and girls, for example, from telling sexist jokes or sending sexist memes, catfishing, sending unsolicited porn to stalking and electronic surveillance. Technology facilitated gender harm refers to information and communication technology than causes harm to women and girls. (See M – Misogyny).

- Online **racist hate** occurs when words or actions are used to discriminate or disadvantage people because of their colour, race, nationality, culture or ethnic origins (see R – Racism).
- Hate and prejudice against **LGBTQ+ communities** including homophobia (hate against someone who identifies as gay or lesbian), biphobia (hate against those who identify as bisexual) and transphobia (hate against those who are transgender).
- **Ableism and disablism** refers to hate linked to an individual's disability. Online, disablism refers to hate which targets those with physical or mental health disability and ableism refers to online hate that focuses on those who are able-bodied.

What are the characteristics of online hate?

Online hate can manifest in many different forms, some of which include:

- **Hate speech** which can include derogatory language, slurs or threats which discriminates against individuals or groups. Hate speech can spread quickly across social media and the internet and can reach large audiences.
- **Misinformation** which is false or inaccurate information that is spread over the internet accidentally which can present false narratives or perpetuate stereotypes and discrimination. **Disinformation** refers to sharing this false information deliberately.
- **Excluding** certain groups from online spaces can marginalise individuals or communities.

- Bullying online **(cyberbullying)** can include persistent online harassment or intimidation of others, for example, sending threatening, intimidating or abusive texts, images and videos and even trolling.
- Online **dehumanisation** refers to portraying individual people or groups as less than human or inferior which could include spreading harmful stereotypes, calling for or glorifying violence against different groups, through jokes, images or memes that mock or degrade others.

The impact of online hate

Online hate can have serious consequences on children and young people including their mental health, academic impact and behaviour. They can feel angry, frightened and upset whether this is directed at them personally or at others. Online hate can also result in a child feeling lonely, anxious and depressed with feelings of low self-esteem and self-worth. Persistent exposure to hateful content can lead to longer term psychological trauma. It can also have an impact on a child's behaviour who may respond to online hate through anger or even by withdrawing from situations and activities. In the classroom, online hate may lead to children and young people removing themselves from a learning setting due to fear of encountering more hate. The distress caused by online hate could also impact on their academic performance.

Encourage your child to be their best online self, by:

- Thinking before making or liking a comment, sharing an image or sending a message.
- Treating others online how you would want to be treated yourself.
- Considering other people's feeling with kindness and empathy.
- Don't say something online that you wouldn't say face to face.
- Reaching out to others to ask and offer support.
- Embracing and respecting individual different points of view from different backgrounds so that you can see a balanced view of the world which spreads positivity and kindness.

Views of parents, carers and professionals on online hate

Some parents shared their concerns about online hate. One parent said,

> *"There just seems to be a lot of hate and unkindness online. The more you look the more you find. If it jumps out at me, how much hate are my children seeing online, because they are constantly on their screens."*

Another parent reflected that:

> *"It was through silly memes… they were supposed to be funny but they were offensive and racist. They were afraid of saying it to my daughters but thought it was ok to put it on social media where all her friends could see."*

Some teachers reflected on the impact of online hate and identified the need for further support. One teacher said:

> *"We are just not equipped with the knowledge or the tools to help combat online hate. We know it's there but we need more training and support."*

Another said:

> *"It's hard to know how to tackle online hate. I worry about extremism and bullying, but sometimes class discussions can be really challenging".*

Practical TIPS Practical tips on supporting your child to tackle and prevent online hate

There are many ways to support children and young people to tackle and prevent hate in online spaces, some of which include:

- **Protect yourself and others** – set up parental controls and block anyone causing harm.
- **Resist the urge to respond** to hateful content as this can encourage further dialogue and risk further conflict.
- **Break the algorithm echo chamber** – algorithms are influenced by what and how we engage with social media or video sharing platforms. For those who watch harmful content they will be presented with even more of the same type of content which creates echo chambers. It is important to break out of the echo chamber by encouraging them to change their feeds and hide content. To do this they need to be helped to recognise both hidden and direct online hate.
- Every social media account has different options for how much control users have over their algorithms. You can help your child **reset the algorithms** – explore each of the social media platforms that is popular with your child to find out how to reset algorithms.
- Talk openly with your child about online hate and **change the narrative** – some children and young people may not even realise that they themselves are spreading online hate. Talk to them about the impact of online hate and encourage them not to spread hateful content.
- Explain **what is and what is not ok** by reminding your child know how hurtful and unkind it is to gossip, spread rumours, and bully others online.
- **Parental controls** can help you monitor and limit the time your child spends online and what they do when they are online. Parental controls can be used across WiFi and individual apps and devices.
- **Report it!** Explain to your child that hate crime is illegal and report it through the site where the online hate is taking place. Whilst many apps and sites have moderators in place to help remove harmful content, some do not. Encourage children and young people to report it when they see it!

For further information and support

Stop Hate UK provides training, information and advice and reporting service
www.stophateuk.org

Report online hate crimes on a site developed by **National Police Chiefs' Council** – Report a hate crime – True Vision
report-it.org.uk

Internet Matters
https://www.internetmatters.org/issues/online-hate/

References

Ofcom (2024) *Insights into Children's Digital Use*. Ofcom.

Ofcom (2023) 'Just one in six young people flag harmful content online'. Ofcom.

Ofcom (2025) *Children and Parents: Media and Attitudes Report*. Ofcom.

I – Influencers

The chapter will cover:

- An overview of research on social influencers.
- The influencer industry.
- Different types of influencers.
- The impact of social influencers.
- Views of parents, carers and professionals on social influencers.
- Practical tips and activities to help navigate the world of online influencers.

Introduction

Details of specific influencers have been kept to a minimum, because whilst most promote positive messages, there are those who do not and the negative content they produce, viewed by children and young people, has a significant detrimental impact on their mental health. Therefore, there is limited reference to specific influencers, whose popularity comes and goes, with the aim of not adding to their likes or following.

Many social media influencers have a large and loyal online following and have a big impact on children and young people's social media use. Influencers are people who have established credibility in a specific industry, who have large audiences following them online through gaming or social media. Social media influencers – otherwise known as 'YouTubers', 'bloggers', 'vloggers' or 'gamers' – often try to persuade others to act on their recommendations, can provide information and advice on a specific subject or even offer just entertainment. Many social media influencers are celebrities in their own right.

Research on social influencers

Research suggest that influencers are a key part of children and young people's lives. Ofcom (2024) reports that

- 31% of all social media users follow celebrities.
- 50% of 16–24 year olds share that they follow celebrities online.

Whilst there are influencers who are positive role models, there are others who are not! Research by Internet Matters found, for example, that:

- 23% of 15–16 year old boys, and dads between the age of 25 and 34 years old, had a positive impression of Andrew Tate, an influencer who promotes misogyny content and messaging.

The influencer industry

The social media influencer industry has grown astronomically over the last decade. The global influencer marketing value is $34.2 billion which has tripled since 2020. There are various different types of social media influencers, many of whom are now seen as celebrities or started as celebrities, but many have sponsorship arrangements and are linked to brands to promote products or services in exchange for money or free products for themselves. Social media influencers will have specific interests (for example, health and wellness, fashion, lifestyles, gaming, beauty, travel), and many children and young people now aspire to be a social influencer as a career choice, seeing it as lucrative, fun and offering the ability to gain global popularity.

Social media influencers can build huge audiences and fan bases and are reliant on those who 'follow', 'share', 'like' or 'subscribe' to their posts, videos or images. Images, reels or videos often encourage peer to peer sharing. Many companies rely on social media influencers to sell and recommend products or services as part of their marketing strategies.

Many influencers engage with their audience by promoting themselves as friends and are often considered by young people as relatable and trustworthy, and build a huge following.

Types of influencers

There are different types of social media influencers which are categorised by the number of followers:

- **Mega influencers** – more than 1 million followers (tend to be celebrities).
- **Macro influencers** – 100k to 1 million followers (tend to be social media celebrities and professional bloggers).
- **Micro influencers** – 10k to 100k followers (tend to be social media celebrities with smaller followings).
- **Nano influencers** – 1k to 10k followers (tend to be social media influencers with a small but focused following, usually relating to a specific topic).

There are different categories of influencers based on their interests or contents, which include, for example:

- **Kidfluencers** – influencers are becoming younger and younger, as a new phenomenon of 'kidfluencers' have appeared. These are children usually between the age of 4 and 14 who have an online presence and create views and followings, many of whom have millions of followers. For the really young kidfluencers, parents will often manage their online accounts. Whilst many parents set up accounts for their children to connect with friends and family (known as 'sharenting'), others will manage their children as kidfluencers for commercial gain, to promote products and marketing brands to other parents and children.
- **Family influencers** – parents who create content featuring family life. This includes sharenting, with parents using online platforms to share information about their children.
- **Travel influencers** – capture trips and destinations.
- **Beauty and fashion influencers** – by sharing shopping and beauty tips and the latest trends on clothing, skin, hair and make-up.
- **Fitness and sporting influencers** – share exercises, workouts and sporting tips and experiences.

- **Gaming influencers** – offer game reviews, live-streams and gaming hacks.
- **Lifestyle influencers** – cover overall lifestyle issues including fashion, travel, home décor, wellbeing.
- **Social, political or environmental influencers** – campaign and promote different causes
- **Food influencers** – sharing recipes or food and shopping tips.
- **Day-in-the-life influencers** – share content of their daily routines.
- **'Get ready with me' influencers (GRWM)** – share their preparation routines including getting dressed, putting on make-up or doing their hair.
- **Health and wellness influencers** – with young people accessing health information through social media, influencers potentially play a key part in providing content on exercise, fitness, mental health and general etc.
- **Adult content influencer** – adult entertainers often stemming from Only Fans, influencers can also include 'shock' influencers.

What is the impact of social media influencers?

Whether your child is watching beauty tutorials or learning new gaming skills, many social media influencers act as role models and promote positive self-esteem, body image, financial awareness, ethical values and positive mental wellbeing. However, some social media influencers can promote toxic views and behaviours amongst children and young people. As poor role models, some can promote risk-taking behaviours, through hate speech, false information and online social manipulation. For many children and young people, influencers are seen as relatable, like friends, because they interact with them frequently. Many aim to strike a personal connection with their audience. Some children and young people can develop their identity by comparing themselves to social media influencers which becomes dangerous when online images are often doctored, false, fake or misleading.

Parents, carers and professionals' views on social influencers

Parents and professionals noted the impact of influencers through social media. One parent said:

"When I asked my daughter why she followed X (social media influencer), she said, 'because I want to be like her – she is thin, beautiful and all my friends like her'".

A teacher advised students to:

"block inappropriate material and messages spread by influencers. We need to stop influencers posting lifestyle advice that is damaging and affects students' mental health especially about diet, body shape and exercise."

Practical **TIPS**

Practical tips on navigating the world of social media influencers

There are a number of ways for you to help children and young people navigate the world of online influencers. The most important thing is to help your child objectively discuss the role of influencers:

- **Be curious!** Find out which influencers your child and their friends follow and why. Why not ask "How does watching this influencer make you feel?" and "Why do you and/or your friends follow this influencer?"
- Encourage **critical thinking** by discussing the authenticity and impact of the messages that are shared by any social influencer. Why not ask "Does this influencer reflect real life?" or "Do you think this influencer is a good role model for young people?"
- Discuss the **positives and negatives** of different influencers by exploring what messages are being conveyed and whether they appear real and authentic?
- Encourage exposure to influencers that portray a **positive role model** (for example, those that promote positive mental wellbeing or environmental causes)
- Why not **follow the influencers** that your child subscribes to, so that you know more about them and the values that they promote?

Activities

These activities have been created to help children and young people understand the influence of social media influencer, critically analyse the online content that they promote and reflect on their own values and online behaviour. These activities can be delivered with both individual and groups of children and young people.

1. Spot the positive influencer role models

When discussing influencers with your child(ren), can you both identify ten well-known influencers and what they actively promote? Discuss whether they promote positive or negative messages to others.

2. Influencer impact challenge

Create profiles for six real and six fictional influencers with different types of content (e.g. gaming, fashion, beauty etc) and include:

- Name of influencer
- Content focus
- Follower amount
- Engagement style
- An example of a recent post

Discuss each of the influencers and determine:

- What audience is the influencer targeting?
- What values is the influencer promoting? (e.g. are they authentic, kind, empathetic?)
- How does the influencer's content affect the audience? Does it have a positive or negative impact?

3. Create your own fictional social media influencer

Encourage your child(ren) to design their own fictional social media influencer and think about:

- What is their personality like?
- What do they look like?
- What is the influencers topic of interest? (e.g. environmental, gaming, beauty, gardening etc)
- Create a slogan for the influencer
- Create a draft social media post

References

Internet Matters (2023) *"It's really easy to go down that path" Young people's experiences of online misogyny and image-based abuse.* Internet Matters (ref Andrew Tate).

Lim, M.S.C., Molenaar, A., Brennan, L., Reid, M. & McCaffrey, T. (2022) Young adults' use of different social media platforms for health information: insights from web-based conversations. *J Med Internet Res* 24 (1) e23656 (reference to health influencers).

Ofcom (2024) *Adults' Media Use and Attitudes Report*. Ofcom.

Statistica (2024) 'Influencer marketing worldwide – statistics and facts'. Statistica Research Department www.statistica.com

J – Joy and fear of missing out

The chapter will cover:

- An overview of the research on the joy and fear of missing out.
- What is meant by both the fear and joy of missing out.
- Practical tips and activities to turn the fear of missing out into a joy of missing out.

FOMO or JOMO?

The Joy Of Missing Out (JOMO) refers to the positive feelings from intentionally disconnecting from the digital world and being 'present' in the moment. This is different to the Fear Of Missing Out (FOMO) which results in feelings of anxiety when withdrawing from the digital world. With children and young people spending more and more time attached to their online devices, the need to remind both ourselves and them of the benefits of disconnecting from the digital world has never been more important. This is about ensuring that not only do we encourage children and young people to break the habit of reaching for the phone to fill time, out of pure habit or for the fear of missing out but we also note our own feelings of FOMO!

Research on the joy and fear of missing out

Research (Hunt, 2018) found that reducing time spent on social media impacts on FOMO. It identified that limiting time spent on social media by at least 30 minutes significantly reduces FOMO and anxiety. Research also suggests that following influencers is one of the reasons for FOMO, by not wanting to miss out on what is happening in the life of an influencer and this leads to the pressure of returning to social media. As well as this, Chan *et al* (2022) also states that adopting more mindful social media use can help turn FOMO into JOMO without the need to disconnect from social media platforms entirely. They introduce social media mindfulness practice (SMMP) as a way of encouraging those who use social media to reflect on their motivations, emotions and habits when using social media platforms.

What is digital FOMO?

Fear of missing out could be the feeling that others are having more fun, living better lives, have more friends than you, as well as the fear of missing relevant news or information. Digital FOMO can result in the need to stay connected online and engaged with social media. This can lead to excessive digital consumption which can potentially affect mental wellbeing and physical health. (See E – Excessive use.)

What is digital JOMO?

The joy of missing out (JOMO) can ultimately provide feelings of freedom and positivity from not being constantly online and tied to our digital devices. The image below identifies seven key examples of elements linked to the digital joy of missing out which you can share with your child:

1. **Mindful disconnection** refers to the conscious and purposeful disconnection with technology to undertake other mindful and positive activities which do not rely on being online. Thomas (2023) refers to how new hobbies are a great way to disconnect from social media rather than using social media purely for entertainment or passing the time.
2. Finding **joy in being present** by noticing current surroundings, what you feel and how your body reacts by being offline. Hence, living in the moment and appreciating where you are rather than seeking comparison with others and what they are doing.
3. Prioritising activities which **nurture your physical and emotional wellbeing** e.g. spending time in nature, playing sports or reading.

4. Focusing on intentional and **mindful living** by making sure that offline activities align with your goals and personal aspirations and what matters to you most.
5. Embrace **real life** by engaging in situations and activities in person and away from technology can help your child appreciate the 'here and now'.
6. **Increased self-awareness** which helps us reflect on how our activities affect our mood and feelings.
7. Enhanced and improved **meaningful real-life relationships** and human connections. When children and young people have fulfilled relationships and interactions with others, they feel valued and supported and are less likely to seek external validation from social media.

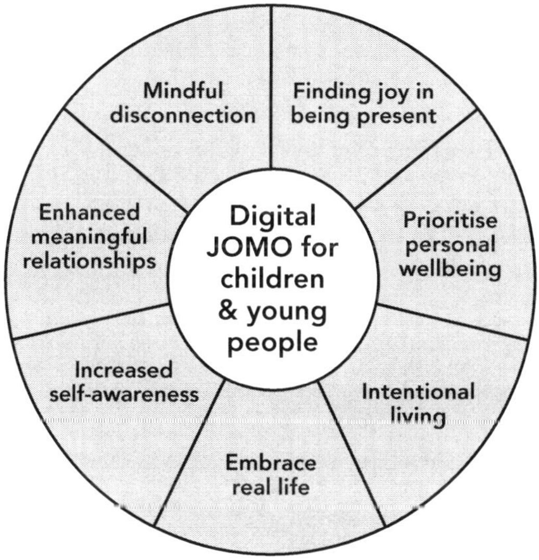

Figure 9: Seven key elements associated to digital JOMO amongst children and young people.

Practical TIPS — Practical tips to support your child to turn FOMO into JOMO

Practical tips to help turn your child's fear of missing out online into a joy of missing out by helping them consider the benefits of how meaningful real-life experiences and online disconnection can bring joy and positivity which include:

- Focus on **quality time** by encouraging your child to engage in activities away from the screen and help them appreciate living in the present.
- **Model healthy digital behaviour** which includes the benefits of JOMO by showing your child the benefits of being present and the joy of doing activities offline. Why not pursue some of these activities together?
- Try to **limit screentime** exposure by taking digital breaks or agreeing screen use at certain times.
- Encourage the importance of building strong and **meaningful (in person) friendships** offline to help build social and emotional resilience and feelings of belonging.
- Discuss the difference between **reality and perceived reality** and how social media can portray a distorted version of reality and other people's lives which can enhance the fear of missing out.

Activities to help turn FOMO into JOMO

There are various activities to explore with children and young people to help cultivate a better relationship with social media and celebrate the joy of missing out. For example:

- Have a **family digital detox day or unplugged evenings** (see E – Excessive Use) to purposefully disconnect from all screens and focus on offline activities instead
- Write a **JOMO journal** to celebrate how it feels to be disconnected from social media and focus on areas of gratitude. Encourage your child to identify the things that they have enjoyed doing away from their screens and what they felt whilst doing these activities. This will help your child focus on meaningful activities rather than what is missing from their life
- Explore practising **mindfulness** together to help remind you and your child of the importance and impact of being present
- Participate in some fun **activities together** – go on a walk and reconnect with nature or play a game

For further information and advice

Young Minds – offers resources and a parent helpline to support children's mental health, including anxiety linked to social media and peer pressure (www.youngminds.co.uk)

Parentzone – provides guidance to parents on digital resilience, helping families navigate the impact of online pressures (www.parentzone.org.uk)

References

Chan, S. *et al* (2022) Social media and mindfulness: From the fear of missing out (FOMO) to the joy of missing out (JOMO). *Journal of Consumer Affairs*, 56 (3) 1312–1331.

Hunt, M.G., Marx, R., Lipson, C. & Young, J. (2018) No more FOMO: limiting social media decreases loneliness and depression. *Journal of the Society of Clinical Psychologists*, 37 (10) 751–768.

Social media: influencers and FOMO. INM Marketing Group. Accessed September 29, 2022. https://inm-group.com/social-media-influencers-and-FOMO

Thomas, I. (2022) The essential art of disconnecting: why it's so important. Psychologs.

K – Keep learning

The chapter will cover:

- An overview of research on learning and digital wellbeing.
- Learning at home and school using digital media.
- Whole school approach to digital wellbeing.
- Practical tips for parents and carers to support your child's digital learning at home.

Creating a home learning environment

The use of online devices and platforms are key to enabling and facilitating children and young people's learning. Children learn in an online world through a mix of digital tools, resources, interactive experiences and by connecting with others. This chapter will identify the importance of thriving online by focusing on learning at home and at school or college. It focuses on the importance of a safe and dedicated home learning environment and provides practical tips for helping create one. It also identifies how a whole school and college approach to digital wellbeing is fundamental to creating a healthy digital learning environment. It includes creating supportive environments to promote digital literacy and safety, the role of leaderships and governance, embedding digital wellbeing in the teaching curriculum and the active engagement of pupils, parents and staff.

Research on learning and digital wellbeing

Research shows that parents believe that digital devices can help children to keep learning. The *Children and Parents: Media Use and Attitudes Report* (Ofcom, 2024) identified that 71% of parents of children aged 3 to 17 found being online helped their children:

- With schoolwork (71%).
- To develop skills with reading and numbers (54%).
- To find out about the news (32%).

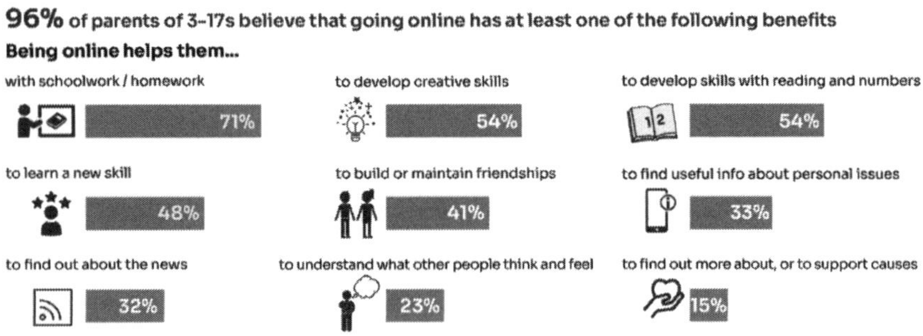

Figure 10: Parent's views of the benefits of being online (*Children and Parents: Media Use and Attitudes Report* © Ofcom 2024)

More children are watching videos which help them with their schoolwork or to learn new things. Nearly half of children aged 13 to 17 who watch videos via sites or apps are now watching videos on video-sharing platforms that help them learn new things or help them with their schoolwork (Ofcom, 2025). Ofcom also recognised that children and young people are starting to access AI technology to help them learn more, with over a third (35%) of 8- to 17-year-old users of AI stating that they used it to learn at home and 37% used it at school. This reflects a growing trend in how children and young people are informally and formally integrating AI into their every-day learning..

However, the same report also highlighted the impact of digital disadvantage which has significant impact on a child's learning. A third of school children don't have continuous access to an appropriate learning device and their ability to learn at home is compromised. This includes 55% of these children accessing parents' devices to learn and 12% borrowing them from other people, school or other organisations.

Access to digital learning

Home is a key educational learning environment and having access to digital technology and a comfortable and safe space will allow children and young people to engage in learning activities and promote positive digital wellbeing. For many, home is a place where children and young people learn, whether it is through informal learning through access to social media, gaming or the internet or formally through completing school/college work.

However, it is important to recognise that digital disadvantage for some families impacts on their access to digital technology and poor digital literacy skills. Children without continuous access to the internet or devices can miss out on accessing homework platforms and learning portals which ultimately can affect their access to education.

For those children and young people where emotional factors lead to school refusal or avoidance, the need to keep learning at home is imperative. It is important to create a healthy and safe digital home learning space so that they can learn and stay connected with others.

Whole school and college approach to digital wellbeing

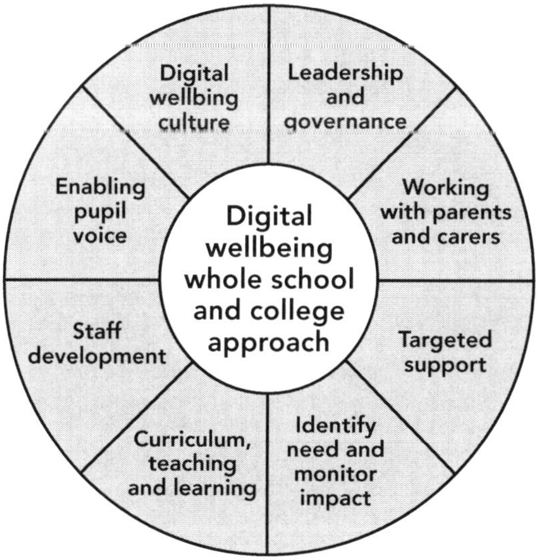

Figure 11: The digital wellbeing whole school and college approach principles

In the UK, schools and colleges are required to support digital wellbeing through a range of legal and policy frameworks. Under *Keeping Children Safe in Education* (Department of Education, 2023) schools must protect pupils from online harm and have effective monitoring and safeguarding procedures. The RSHE (2019) curriculum makes it mandatory to teach online safety, screentime and the impact of social media on mental health. Schools also have the responsibility under the Data Protection Act (2018) to safeguard pupil's digital privacy.

The online lives of children and young people exist at school and college where digital wellbeing is fundamental. Creating a whole school and college approach to promote digital wellbeing focuses on the need to support staff and pupils; strengthening the ethos and environment; leadership which promotes digital safety and wellbeing; and a curriculum that embeds digital literacy and learning. Public Health England's 8 principles of the whole school and college approach (2023) can be adapted to promote digital wellbeing.

1. **Leadership and governance**
    a. Both school and college leadership and governors should champion the whole school or college digital wellbeing as well as online safety.
    b. Ensure all staff, parents and pupils are aware of key laws and regulations that impact on digital wellbeing (e.g. Data Protection and Privacy Laws, Keeping Children Safe in Education, Acceptable Use Policies etc). Embed digital wellbeing within all school policies.
    c. Schools and colleges should be encouraged to have an elected digital lead governor and digital wellbeing lead on senior management team.
2. **Staff development**
    d. Ensure that staff have the tools to support their own digital wellbeing as well as their pupils. This could include receiving training on digital literacy, technical skills, online safety as well as digital wellbeing.
    e. All school staff including teaching, teaching assistants and facilities staff should feel confident in identifying online harms and supporting pupils who are impacted by digital harm.
    f. Staff should model good digital citizenship as role models within the educational setting.

3. **Digital wellbeing ethos and environment**

    g. Ensure that there is a positive school and college digital wellbeing culture which promotes a safe, healthy and responsible environment for not only pupils but also staff, parents and carers. This includes making sure digital tools support learning and promotes good behaviour and positive digital wellbeing.

    h. Encourage staff, parents and carers modelling positive digital engagement and pupils feel encouraged to speak up if there is poor digital behaviour.

4. **Curriculum, teaching and learning**

    i. Embed digital wellbeing into the curriculum is essential by teaching pupils about online digital safety, digital resilience, digital literacy and technology use.

    j. This can be through the dedicated relationships, sex and health education curriculum but also needs to be included throughout the wider curriculum.

5. **Pupil voice**

    k. It is imperative to help understand the digital wellbeing needs of pupils and ensuring that it is reflected in the mental health and wellbeing vision, design and implementation of the digital wellbeing whole school and college approach.

    l. Pupil's voice should be involved in shaping policies and initiatives that impact on digital wellbeing.

    m. A school or college could create a digital wellbeing pupil council or digital wellbeing ambassadors to support and promote this approach.

6. **Partnership with parents, carers and the community**

    n. Working with and listening to parents and carers is essential to ensure the mental health and emotional wellbeing of pupils. It is important to support the digital wellbeing and literacy of parents and carers.

    o. This could be achieved by developing a digital wellbeing guide or running digital wellbeing workshops on a range of topics (e.g. online safety, cyberbullying, online harms, misogyny, healthy digital relationships, digital literacy etc) and helping to support their own and their child's digital experience online.

p. It is important to recognise digital disadvantage for those parents and carers who lack the skills or devices to support their child to thrive online and help address this by offering access to equipment, resources and skill development.

7. **Targeted support**

q. For those with identified specific digital wellbeing needs, a school or college should collaborate with other organisations to provide appropriate support, for example, school nurses, local voluntary or community organisations, education psychologists, and CAMHS.

8. **Identifying need and evaluating impact**

r. It is good practice to regularly evaluate whether the approach is making an impact on positive digital wellbeing. It is important to ensure that the needs of pupils, staff, parents and carers are being met.

s. This can be undertaken through whole school or college surveys or hearing from pupils, staff and parents to find out what their concerns are and how the school or college can support them.

Parents, carers and professionals' views of learning

The importance of learning to promote digital wellbeing was highlighted by parents and teachers who recognised that:

> *"There are many educational opportunities online. For example, learning another language, hearing the news, help with schoolwork" and "the breadth of online learning that is available benefits all styles of learning. We all learn at difference paces and in different ways. Online learning in its different forms can tailor abilities with a proactive learning experience".*

However, the challenges with learning and digital wellbeing were also noted:

> *"Not all of our pupils have access to the right equipment. We know that we have pupils that if we set certain homework, some say that they have to do it on their mum's phone which we know is completely inappropriate and not safe".*

Practical TIPS — Practical tips for parents and carers to support your child's digital learning at home

It is important to work with your child to help create a healthy and safe digital home learning environment. For those households who do not have all the equipment and resources to help create a dedicated home learning space, liaise with your child's school or college to see how they can support you. Ways in which you can create a dedicated healthy learning environment include:

- Finding a **quiet space** with as many distractions removed as possible to help a child stay focused.
- **Balance screentime** with other activities – take a break and seek an alternative activity which is less sedentary.
- Ensure appropriate **lighting** is available including natural light or additional lighting if required.
- Help your child ensure the space is **organised** and free from clutter.
- Make sure the space is **safe and comfortable** (but not too comfortable as you may fall asleep!).
- Stock up the space with relevant **supplies** e.g. charger, access to WiFi, power, stationery.

For more information and advice

Internet Matters provides top tips for online learning https://www.internetmatters.org/advice/by-activity/learning-online-a-guide-for-parents/top-tips-for-online-learning/

References

Department for Education (2023) *Keeping Children Safe in Education*. DfE.

Data Protection Act (2018)

Department for Education (2019) *Relationships Education, Relationships and Sex Education and Health Education: Statutory Guidance for Governing Bodies, Proprieters, Head Teachers, Principals, Senior Leaders Teams, Teachers*. DfE.

Ofcom (2024) *Children and Parents: Media Use and Attitudes Report*. Ofcom.

Ofcom (2025) *Children and Parents: Media Use and Attitudes Report*. Ofcom.

Office for Health Improvement and Disparities and Department for Health (2023) *Promoting Children and Young People's Mental Health and Wellbeing: Guidance on the 8 Principles of a Whole School and College Approach to Promoting Mental Health and Wellbeing*. OHID/DH.

L – Digital literacy

The chapter will cover:

- An overview of research on digital literacy.
- Types of digital literacy skills that enable children to use digital technology confidently, critically and responsibly.
- Views of parents, carers and professionals on digital literacy.
- Practical tips and activities to support digital literacy.

What is digital literacy?

Keeping up to date with the online world at the same speed as children and young people can be intimidating and daunting. Digital literacy is key to help with our digital parenting, but it is also essential for children and young people to be able to thrive in an ever-evolving digital world. Digital literacy refers to the skills needed to understand and use digital technology safely and effectively in order to support and protect children and young people in the online world. It is not just about knowing how to practically use digital tools and technology, but it is also about being able to use them safely, confidently and appropriately. Our role as parents and professionals is to help children and young people navigate the digital landscape both safely and responsibly but for many of us, we need to equip ourselves with better digital literacy skills.

Research on digital literacy

Digital disadvantage is a key barrier for children and young people's access to the online world. Lack of access to digital devices and the internet as well as low levels of digital skills leads to digital disadvantage. The Good Things Foundation (2024) found that in the UK, 3.7 million families are below the minimum digital living standard with 8.5 million lacking basic digital skills and 0.6 million young people lacking access to home internet or a suitable device. Those families who are likely to be most affected from digital disadvantage include:

- Those from low-income, rural or underserved areas.
- Those experiencing insecure housing.
- Minority ethnic groups.
- Those children and young people with special educational needs.

For some children and their families, the key barriers are having access to and affording reliable and up to date devices (eg smartphone, laptop or tablets) or dependable WiFi (Ofcom, 2025). This can affect children and young people's social interaction, access to learning and ultimately their mental wellbeing.

The *Children and Parents: Media and Attitudes Report* (Ofcom, 2024) found that over a third of school children do not have access to a device at home for online learning which included 44% of primary school aged children and 19% of secondary school children. This resulted in over half (55%) of the children within these families sharing devices, and 12% borrowing a device from the school or another organisation.

Worryingly, Internet Matters (2024) found that children and young people do not have the digital literacy skills to keep themselves safe. They found that 42% of children 3 to 17 years old did not know how to set up privacy settings and 31% did not know how to block an account with over half of children unaware of how to report content or users. This was in comparison to 36% of parents being unaware of social media privacy settings, and 55% not aware of safe search settings. Parents were seen as having a vital role in children's digital lives as they were identified as the key source of information on online safety by 83% of children. This makes it even more imperative to equip both parents, carers and children with the right skills and knowledge to help them navigate the online world safely and responsibly.

What are key digital literacy skills?

Figure 12: Types of digital literacy skills for parents, carers and professionals

There are a number of key digital literacy skills for parents, carers and professionals to help themselves and children and young people navigate the digital world, seven examples of which include:

1. Positive netiquette

Digital etiquette (netiquette) refers to online kindness, respect and empathy and by helping your child understand how their actions and language online affect others is fundamental. This includes not only online language but also being aware of the tone of language used to help avoid misunderstanding and the importance of avoiding spamming or trolling others. Being a role model and leading by example shows any child or young person how to communicate with respect and kindness online.

2. Digital communication and language skills

Digital communication encompasses the ability to communicate, to share ideas and information and interact with others. Being aware of online language (including online slang and emojis) and terminology and how it can be misinterpreted or misunderstood is really important. Encourage your child to think before they click!

3. Online safety

Build your own online safety knowledge and skillset to promote your child and your own understanding of cyber security, how to protect personal information and online identity. This Guide reiterates a number of practical ways to help develop both your child and your online safety skills. (See O – Online Safety).

4. Digital technical skills

Having basic technical and practical skills to understand the use of digital tools, equipment and sites is fundamental. Explore the many tools or information online available to help enhance and build your skills.

5. Critical thinking skills

It is important to teach your child to critically evaluate what they see or hear online, how to make informed decisions and question the credibility of digital platforms, content and sites. There is a lot of online content that isn't always true or exaggerated, so being able to critically assess what is inappropriate, untrue and what is fake news is key. (See F – Fake news.)

6. Cultural digital skills

Being able to help your child navigate and engage in digital technology in a culturally sensitive and appropriate way is fundamental. This includes engaging respectfully online with different cultures and being aware that digital platforms shape cultural trends and identities. It is also about having the skills to recognise and navigate away from sites and content that promote online hate (see H – Online hate), including racism (see R – Racism) and misogyny (see M – Misogyny).

7. Digital kindness skills

Digital kindness is an essential skill that helps children and young people build respect, empathy and positive relationships online. Helping children consider the language and tone of their communication online is fundamental. Ensuring they celebrate diversity in digital spaces and that they ask for consent before sharing any content is important.

Views from parents, carers and professionals on digital literacy

Many parents and teachers referred to the importance of educating themselves and advised others to:

> *"make sure you stay as up to date as you can with emerging trends with regards to chatrooms, websites and apps"*

> *"There are many risks and ever-changing platforms, so it is difficult to be fully up-to-date and informed enough or feel confident enough to speak with any knowledge to my children".*

Parents in particular referred to their lack of digital literacy and that the:

> *"kids know more than we do, so sometimes it's hard to help them or know what is harmful and what isn't".*

> *"I am baffled and scared to use AI… .I haven't got a clue how to use it."*

Other parents talked about their fear of technology which was referred to as one parent as:

> *"the need to be proactive to learn about technology and not be fearful and sticking our heads in the sand because it is all too alien to us. We need to equip ourselves with the digital skills and knowledge to help our children rather than be in constant fear of the negative aspect of the online world and not knowing how it works".*

Professionals highlighted the importance of maintaining open dialogue with children and young people saying:

> *"Take an interest in their digital use and ask questions. Don't assume it's all negative".*
>
> *"Allow time for their digital use, so it doesn't encourage them to be online secretly."*

Another professional reflected on the importance to:

> *"empower parents and professionals to become good digital citizens, to provide them with the digital skills to help them see that digital technology can be a tool as well as a weapon".*

Practical TIPS

Practical tips to support children's digital literacy

Whilst this Guide provides a wealth of practical advice to enhance digital literacy skills, there are additional tips and reminders that should be considered, including:

- Learn how to set up and implement **parental controls and privacy settings**. Help ensure that both your and your child's social media profiles are private.
- **Review your digital skills** and build on them to help you become better connected with the online world. There are a number of online tools that can assess your digital skill level and help you learn.
- Talk with your child and encourage online respectful and kind digital behaviour and language. Discuss the importance of **netiquette** and how their behaviour and language impacts on their online interactions with other people.
- Remind your child of how their **digital footprint** is relatively permanent and can impact on their online and offline reputation.

Often, if photos, images and comments are shared online, it is easy to lose control of where they end up as they can be copied, changed and shared without your child knowing.

Digital literacy activities

Three activities have been developed for you to complete with children and young people to help improve digital literacy:

1. Coloured heart emoji quiz (targeting those working with teenagers)
2. Emoji quiz (targeting those working with teenagers)
3. Digital literacy assessment for parents

All of these resources are available to download and print in full colour online: **https://pavpub.com/mental-health/a-to-z-guide-to-children-and-young-peoples-digital-mental-health-resources**

1. Coloured heart emoji quiz

The use of coloured heart emojis varies and often means different things to different people. They are used to symbolise or emphasise different emotions when communicating, mostly through social media. They often can be used for fun, to save time, to emphasise emotions or to hide the meaning from others.

Test your knowledge of the meanings behind coloured heart emojis – how many different heart emojis are you aware of? What are their meanings?

Note that this emoji quiz is targeted at those living or working with teenagers rather than younger children.

Meanings of coloured heart emojis – answers
Everyone uses emojis in different ways and as a result they have different meanings for different people. The definitions used here are examples only and may have a number of different meanings. The coloured hearts can be defined as (although your child may have different meanings for them!):

Blue heart	Friendship and support
Purple heart	Sexual attraction and passion, feeling horny
Orange heart	Reassurance and "you're going to be ok"
Yellow heart	Mutual interest
Classic red heart	Love or deep friendship
White heart	Someone passing away, peace
Pink heart	Interested but without sex
Black heart	Sadness, dark humour or grief (also Support for Black Lives Matters)
Broken heart	Broken up with someone or missing someone
Heart with a bow	In a relationship with someone
Flaming heart	"You set my heart on fire" or "look amazing"
Pulsating heart	Vibing
Heart that is growing	"My love for you is growing"
Red heart in pink square	Intense friendship
Red heart with a bandage around it	Recovering from a broken heart or break up

2. Emoji quiz (targeting parents, carers and professionals working with teenagers)

Children and young people often use emojis especially through social media to reinforce what they are saying, provide expression to what is being said, for speed, for fun or even for secrecy. Most of the time their meanings are harmless. However, for some emojis there are some concerning hidden meanings which parents, carers and professionals should be aware of.

Note that this emoji quiz is targeted at those living or working with teenagers rather than younger children.

Test your knowledge of the meanings behind emojis – how many of these emojis are you aware of and what are their meanings?

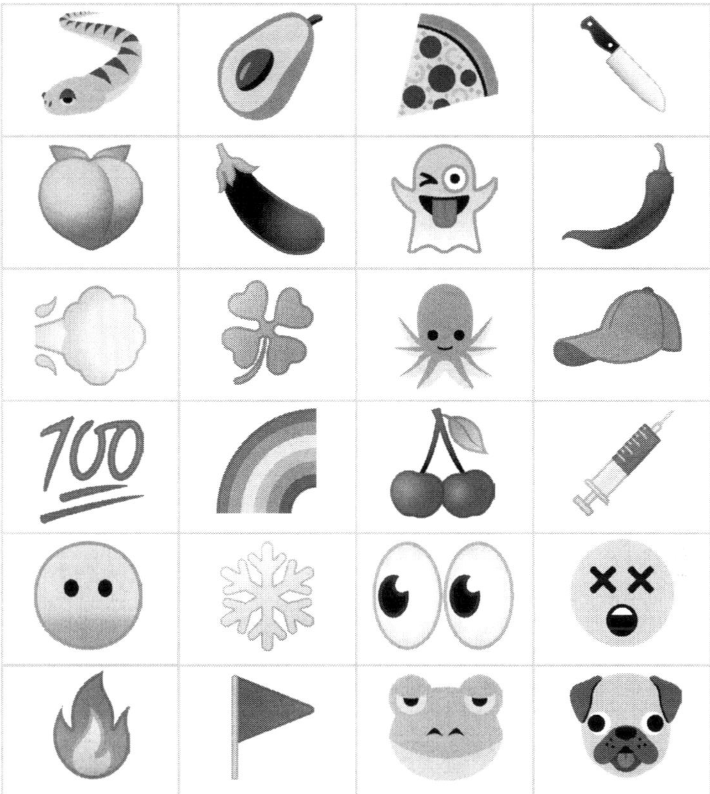

Emojis have a number of meanings which mean different things to different people. The definitions used here are examples only and may have a number of different meanings. Meanings behind the emojis can include (although note that your child may have different definitions for each emoji):

	snake	Backstabber or traitor, penis
	avocado	Basic, vegan food
	slice pizza	I love you or child pornography

	knife	Bad mood
	peach	Buttocks (bum)
	aubergine	Penis
	ghost	Ghost or ignore
	chilli	Spicey, risky or sexy
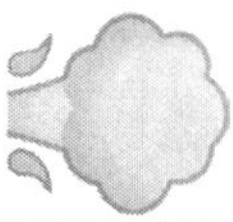	Puff of smoke	Smoking or vaping
	leaf	Marijuana (weed)
	octopus	Cuddles
	cap	A lie or untruth
	100%	Keeping it real or I agree or someone expressing that they are an incel
	rainbow	LGBTQ+

	cherries	Breasts
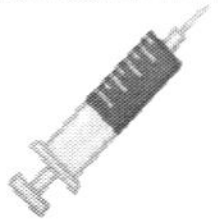	needle	Getting a tattoo, drugs
	Face with no mouth	Keep quiet or don't tell anyone, speechless
	snowflake	Someone who is weak or overly sensitive, cocaine
	eyes	Checking something out or being watched, someone sexy
	Face with cross on the eyes	Just saw something x rated or inappropriate
	fire	Someone who is attractive
	Red flag	Warning about bad behaviour or toxic relationship
	frog	Ugly
	dog	Bitch

3. Digital literacy assessment for parents

This is an activity to explore the digital mental health literacy skills of parents.

This activity will help parents informally assess their digital mental health literacy skills by exploring their knowledge, skills and confidence levels.

1. I know where to find helpful mental health and wellbeing to support my child:

   a. information and advice on the internet?

   b. services on the internet?

2. I feel confident using the mental health and wellbeing resources and information on the internet to support my child's mental health needs.
3. I know where to find helpful mental health and wellbeing apps to support my child's mental health.
4. I am confident using mental health apps to support my child's mental health.
5. I am aware of the different social media platforms available to children and young people.
6. I know how to make sure that a website or app which supports children and young people's mental health is reliable and quality assured?

If the answers to these questions identify that you do not feel confident or have limited digital mental health literacy skills or understanding to be able to support your child thrive online, take time to explore this book further to improve your skills and understanding. Most importantly, engage in open discussions with your child regularly about where and what technology (including digital devices, apps, games social media platforms, and websites) they use, which ones are important to them and why.

For more information and support

Internet Matters provides free interactive digital literacy lessons for teachers and parents to help children aged 9–11. https://www.internetmatters.org/schools-esafety/digital-matters-online-learning-platform/

Digital Literacy Trust provides information on digital literacy and technology and a list of alternative trusted sources of news https://literacytrust.org.uk/information/what-is-literacy/literacy-and-digital-technology/

References

Ofcom (2024) *Children and Parents: Media and Attitudes Report*. Ofcom.

Ofcom (2025) *Exploring Digital Disadvantage: Ofcom Response to Research Findings*. Ofcom.

Good Things Foundation (2024) *Digital Nation 2024*. Good Things Foundation. https://www.goodthingsfoundation.org/policy-and-research/research-and-evidence/research-2024/digital-nation

Internet Matters (2024) *November 2024 Tracker Survey: Insights into Children's Digital Use*. Internet Matters. www.internetmatters.org

M – Misogyny

The chapter will cover:

- An overview of research on misogyny.
- What is misogyny?
- Online misogyny through influencers and content creators.
- Impact of misogyny on mental health.
- Views of parents, carers and professionals.
- Practical tips on how to prevent and tackle online misogyny.

What is misogyny?

Misogyny refers to the fundamental dislike, prejudice against or hatred of women and girls and can occur both in person and online. Misogyny can spread easily online, especially through social media. It can manifest in many different ways online, some of which include:

- **Hate speech** – using derogatory language which can also target women based on sexuality, race, or religion (see H – Online hate).
- **Sexual harassment** – including harmful and sexist comments or jokes, images, memes and videos and the use of emojis which reinforce negative stereotypes and normalise harmful attitudes and behaviours towards women and girls.
- **Body shaming** – using digital platforms to criticise or insult someone based on their appearance which could be linked to their body shape, weight, skin etc. (see B – Body image).

- **Doxing** – a form of cyberbullying which involves sharing personal information without consent which could aim at harassment or exploitation of women.
- **Trolling** – provoking or harassing women online often through inflammatory remarks (see T – Trolling).
- **Cyberstalking** – persistent unwanted attention that can often lead to real world harm.
- **Pornography** – objectification of women which can reinforce harmful stereotypes (see X – X-rated).

Online misogyny also impacts LGBTQ+ young people, as the hateful rhetoric often intersects with homophobia and transphobia, creating a compounded environment of discrimination. Misogynistic language and attitudes can marginalize LGBTQ+ children and young people, especially those who identify as female or non-binary, by invalidating their identities and fostering a toxic space that discourages self-expression. These harmful dynamics can impact on mental health, increase feelings of isolation, and reduce access to supportive communities online. For LGBTQ+ children and young people, who often turn to digital spaces to find acceptance and solidarity through peer communities, the prevalence of online misogyny can turn those same spaces into sources of alienation and hostility.

Addressing this issue requires not only combatting misogyny but also fostering inclusive and affirming digital environments where all young people can thrive online.

How does misogyny present online?

Are you aware of hateful and intimidating comments about women and girls on social media and other online spaces? Online gender-based harm includes a number of key areas, including:

- Online domestic abuse (using technology for coercive and controlling behaviour).
- Image-based sexual abuse (non-consensual sharing of images and cyberflashing).
- Online harassment or pile-ons (groups of co-ordinated individuals target a specific woman or girl online through threats, image-based abuse and misogynistic content).
- Misogyny (Ofcom, 2025).

Research on misogyny

Research undertaken by Internet Matters (2025) found that both children and parents believe that the online world exacerbates misogyny. Half of boys and over half of girls (55%) aged 15 to 16 think that the online world makes misogyny worse. However, the research also shows that parents of girls are more likely to think that online misogyny is not a serious problem (20%), in comparison to parents of boys (31%).

Understanding the term

Internet Matters also found that there was limited understanding of the term 'misogyny'. For example, nearly half (46%) of 15 to 16 year olds had little or no understanding of the term compared to 29% who definitely know the meaning of the word. The research found that most children especially younger children, learned about misogyny from their parents, whereas older children found out themselves about misogyny online. The research emphasised that children and young people were less likely to find out about it through their educational setting.

Research undertaken by NASUWT (2024) found that three in five teachers have identified social media as the No.1 cause of negative pupil behaviour. The survey amongst teachers reported that they were subjected to misogyny in the classroom from both parents and pupils. The survey identified that 18% of teachers reported that they had been subjected to misogyny by a pupil and 5% by a parent or carer.

Online misogyny through influencers and content creators

The manosphere is made up of different community groups or manosphere influencers that promote sexism, misogyny and other harmful ideologies and stereotypes of women. Many use social media platforms to share their beliefs and seek followers and those who adhere to these beliefs often focus on masculine identity. Incel refers to an online subculture of people who believe that they are involuntarily celibate, most often men who are unable to find romantic partners, despite wanting to. This extreme online subculture often blames women and the rise of feminism for the reason that they are celibate.

Many of those who adhere to the incel ideology are drawn to the 'black pill' nihilistic theory that they are the only ones who understand that the issue around sex and attraction is 'set' at birth through genetics with nothing that can be done to improve their situation. This set of beliefs often creates resentment and anger which leads to online misogyny and harassment. Some influencers and content creators are linked to these groups and use online platforms to spread misogynistic, harmful content. One such example is a very controversial social influencer Andrew Tate, who is a British/American who gained an online following due to his comments about women. He has been associated with the incel community and accused of promoting misogynistic ideologies online.

It is important to shift mindsets and cultures to promote inspirational examples of positive male role models which both boys and men can look up to. There are a number of positive male role models on social media from those who promote body positivity and men's mental health to those who challenge toxic masculinity and misogyny. It is important to help encourage children and young people to seek out positive male role models through digital media.

The impact of misogyny on mental health

Misogyny can lead to a range of psychological and emotional impacts on women and girl's mental health, self-esteem, body image and anxiety. Through constant exposure to misogynistic online content, women and girls can start to believe negative stereotypes and believe they are inferior which affects self-worth and self-esteem. It can also lead to unrealistic and harmful beauty standards with girls striving for unattainable bodies which can result in distorted body perception and feelings of inadequacy and anxiety.

Parents, carers and professionals' views of misogyny

One parent described her daughter's experience of online misogyny:

> *"My 16 year old daughter told me that she has stopped using (social media) because of the constant hateful sexist comments and opinions that were starting to affect her mental health".*

A teacher shared that:

> *"I have seen an increase in derogatory comments about girls in the playground, but what is deeply concerning is how this manifests online and this is harder for us to see and deal with".*

> *"The online world can breed toxic masculinity and hatred against girls which leads to behaviours playing out in the classroom."*

Practical TIPS — Practical tips on how to prevent and tackle online misogyny

Whilst this is a really important topic to discuss with your child, age-appropriate conversations are encouraged.

- Engage in **open discussions** with your child about misogyny and the effects that it can have on them and others. Help them **spot the warning signs** of online harmful content including upsetting and harmful content and comments by influencers that spread misogynist views, online hate and toxic masculinity.
- Try to **model respect and equality** by speaking respectfully about all genders and avoiding gendered language and challenging gender stereotypes. It is important to set a positive example to value equality and diversity.
- Provide the skills to help children and young people step up and **challenge** the harmful narrative that perpetuates misogyny, only if it is safely ok to do so. Encourage your child to speak out and say "That is not ok" or "What you are saying is upsetting me".
- Check that your child's devices and platforms are **secure and age-appropriate** and that parental controls are being used (see O – Online Safety).
- Encourage your child to **seek support** if they are concerned with any online content that worries them.

- Education settings are encouraged to take a **whole school and college approach to digital wellbeing and misogyny**. For example, not only ensuring that digital wellbeing and misogyny are covered within the curriculum, but also making sure that the school or college updates and creates policies to address gender-based violence and misogyny, promotes a positive culture and ethos by hearing from pupils, parents and staff and ensuring staff are fully trained.

Activities

1. Celebrating positive male social media role models

It is important to shift mindsets and cultures to promote inspirational examples of positive male role models who both boys and men can look up to. There are a number of positive male role models on social media – from those who promote body positivity and men's mental health to those who challenge toxic masculinity and misogyny.

Try to identify the male role models who powerfully and positively present themselves through social media and the impact that this has on supporting self-esteem, self-confidence and positive wellbeing.

It is important to focus on positive male role models rather than those who promote harmful attitudes. Engaging in a conversation about influencers who promote negative views could result in a child seeking more information about these individuals, affect algorithms and potentially expose them to further toxic ideologies.

2. Tackling misogynistic words and language

Misogynistic language through sexist jokes, comments and words can reinforce misogynistic stereotypes and harmful behaviours.

Identify words and phrases used on social media that promote negative gender-biased views and identify a list of positive words to replace them.

Whole school and college approach to tackling and preventing misogyny checklist

Schools and colleges are important settings to help educate, prevent and tackle misogyny. They are required to address online misogyny within existing legal and policy frameworks aimed at safeguarding and promoting equality. The *Keeping Children Safe in Education* Guidance (Department of Education, 2024) states that schools must protect pupils from online harmful content including misogynistic content, as part of their safeguarding duties. The 'Relationships, Sex and Health Education' (RHSE) curriculum makes it statutory to teach about respectful relationships, online content and the impact of harmful stereotypes including gender-based abuse online.

A whole school and college approach to misogyny will allow for a co-ordinated, sustainable and strategic approach. It is important to work with all staff, pupils, parents and the wider community to foster a culture of respect and equality making schools and colleges safer and more inclusive for everyone. The whole school and college approach to tackling misogyny is grounded in the eight principles outlined in the *Promoting children and young people's emotional health and wellbeing framework*, developed by Public Health England (2023).

Why not consider the following elements of a whole school and college approach to misogyny to how your school and college tackles and prevents misogyny and consider future areas of improvement.

Leadership and management

- Ensure all leaders and governors champion the active prevention of misogyny within schools and colleges.
- Policy implementation – develop and enforce clear policies against misogyny, sexism, and harassment. Ensure these policies are communicated to all members of the school or college community including all staff, parents and pupils.

Ethos and culture

- Foster accountability and inclusive cultures rather than focus solely on blame.
- Create safe spaces for staff, parents and pupils to speak up about any incidents that have affected them, and their concerns about misogyny and misogynistic behaviour.

- Promote positive language and behaviour and challenge misogynistic attitudes, behaviour and language.
- Run school campaigns (e.g. zero tolerance) and display positive messages around the school/college to promote diversity and how to tackle gender-based harms.
- Celebrate positive role models – highlight and celebrate achievements of women and non-binary individuals in various fields to counteract stereotypes and inspire students.

Staff development

- Provide continuous training and resources for all school and college staff to recognise and address misogynistic behaviour and attitudes. Equip them with tools to identify and challenge harmful attitudes and support affected pupils.
- Provide safe spaces for all staff to share their concerns and challenges and act upon the concerns raised.

Curriculum and teaching

- Education and awareness – Incorporate lessons on gender equality, respect, and the impact of misogyny into the whole curriculum (not just Relationships, Sexual Health Education). Use workshops, assemblies and guest speakers to educate students and staff about the issue.
- Digital literacy – Teach students about the dangers of online misogyny and how to navigate digital spaces responsibly and safely. Promote responsible and respectful online behaviour and use of language.

Pupil voice

- Encourage students to lead campaigns or clubs that promote gender equality and inclusivity. Peer-led initiatives can be powerful in changing attitudes.
- Engage pupils in shaping and evaluating policies.

Parent and community engagement

- Work with parents, local organisations, and community leaders to reinforce the message of gender equality beyond the school environment (e.g. by providing information, advice and support through a school website, twilight sessions, school newsletters and workshops).

Identify need and monitor impact

- Identify the views of all staff, parents and pupils to understand views and the challenges about gender-based harms. Find out their concerns and engage them in co-creating solutions.
- Regularly assess the effectiveness of anti-misogyny initiatives and adapt strategies and review policies as needed.

Targeted support

- Ensure a safe and confidential reporting mechanism – create safe and confidential ways for students to report incidents of misogyny or harassment. Ensure that reports are taken seriously and acted upon promptly. This helps with culture and ethos.
- Provide additional resources and information on services for those who need additional support.

Further information and support

Internet Matters provides information, support and resources on misogyny. What is misogyny? Guidance for parents and carers | Internet Matters. https://www.internetmatters.org/issues/online-hate/what-is-misogyny/

Internet Matters provides resources on how to talk to your child about misogyny. How to talk about misogyny guide.pdf. https://www.internetmatters.org/wp-content/uploads/2023/03/Internet-Matters-How-to-talk-about-misogyny-interactive-guide-Mar-2023.pdf

Internet Matters help tackle misogyny in schools Misogyny in schools – Guidance for teachers | Internet Matters. https://www.internetmatters.org/issues/online-hate/what-is-misogyny/misogyny-in-schools-guidance-for-teachers/

References

Internet Matters (2023) "It's really easy to go down that path" Young people's experiences of online misogyny and image-based abuse. Internet Matters.

NASUWT (2024) *Teacher Wellbeing Survey 2024*. Available at https://www.nasuwt.org.uk/advice/health-safety/teacher-wellbeing-survey.html

Department for Education (2024) *Keeping Children Safe in Education:Statutory guidance for schools and colleges*. DfE.

Department for Education (2019) *Relationships Education, Relationships and Sex Education and Health Education: Statutory Guidance for Governing Bodies, Proprietors, Head Teachers, Principals, Senior Leaders Teams, Teachers*. DfE.

Public Health England (2023) *Promoting children and young people's emotional health and wellbeing framework*

N – Networking and building healthy relationships online

The chapter will cover:

- An overview of research on online networking.
- Different types of networking including:
  - social networking;
  - employment networking;
  - online dating.
- An outline of the opportunities and challenges for children and young people networking and building and maintaining relationships online.
- Views of parents, carers and professionals on online networking.
- Practical tips and activities to help children and young people build healthy online networks.

Building and maintaining online relationships

The way children and young people build and maintain their relationships using technology has changed over the years, whether keeping in touch with friends, meeting a romantic partner, finding a job or meeting others who have the same hobbies or interests. Social media can help some children and young people build their networks through various online platforms and devices.

Research on networking online

Digital technology is a key component of keeping us connecting and networking. Ofcom (2023) researched online communications amongst children and found that:

- 71% of 11–18 year olds were more confident to communicate online in comparison to 53% of children and young people preferring in person communication.

In addition, Internet Matters (2024) found that:

- 82% of 9–16 year olds used technology to keep in touch with their friends.
- 60% used digital devices and online platforms because it makes them feel part of a group or community.

Parents, carers and professionals' views of children and young people networking online

Parents, carers and professionals expressed a range of opportunities and challenges associated to children and young people networking online. One parent reflected on the positive aspects of online networking saying:

> *"Online platforms can be safe places to communicate, play and share with friends. Online friendships can be just as socially rewarding as in-person friendships. They can be platforms for children to meet other like-minded others with similar interests that they may not find in schools."*

One teacher reflected on the opportunity of networking to "create a community of like-minded people" and another teacher shared that they had:

> *"worked with pupils who felt like social outcasts within their peer groups at school but have made meaningful networks gaming online or meet-ups about a particular interest of theirs they found out about on online forums.... it can be a space for young people to network who are questioning their sexuality or identity .... to safely discover and relate to...... which can help with their self-worth and self-esteem."*

A social worker said:

> *"In my experience, if a child is struggling to make friends in their day-to-day life...it helps to make online connections to their peers that are meaningful and supportive."*

Opportunities and challenges for children and young people networking and building and maintaining relationships online

There are a number of opportunities and challenges for children and young people when networking online. Whilst this list is not exhaustive, it highlights the issues raised by parents and professionals, outlining the majority of risks are associated to safety and the opportunities are linked to social interaction and connectivity.

Opportunities	Challenges
Helps those children and young people who are more anxious in social situations, build confidence and self-esteem through online relationships.	People don't always present their 'true self' online.

Opportunities	Challenges
It can be easier to express feelings online.	Can lead to exposure of online grooming – when children and young people 'talk to' someone who isn't necessarily who they say they are. This can lead to young people being groomed by online sexual predators.
Ability to access friends and peers 24/7.	Some online posts can perpetuate cyber bullying to tease, harm or abuse others.
Can meet others with similar interests or hobbies and build 'online communities'.	Could lead to online blackmail for a young person to make a financial payment to ensure that photos are not made public.
Can lead to employment opportunities through networking online.	Could result in sexual harassment on online platforms.
Can help children keep in touch with their friends.	Can result in feelings of low self-esteem when messages, photos and images are not acknowledged and responded to.
Can help children learn new things about other people and their cultures and countries.	Creates a digital footprint that can be permanent and accessed widely.

Children and young people and social networking

Whilst digital technology should not replace face to face interactions, for most children and young people it plays a fundamental part of their everyday lives. Social networks provide young people with a way of interacting and connecting with others. On social networking sites, young people talk with each other, upload and music and videos and many children and young people will use more than one social networking site.

Practical TIPS: Practical tips to support children and young people to build healthy social networking relationships

A healthy social networking relationship, whether online or not, is based around respect, trust, and setting clear boundaries together. It is important to help children and young people build digital resilience to manage their online relationships. Here are some tips to help your child build healthy digital relationships:

- Talk to your child about the importance of healthy relationships including the positives and negatives.
- Try and be aware of who your child is talking to online by being curious and having open and honest regular discussions with them.
- Agree safe boundaries about what should and shouldn't be shared online (e.g. nudes, photos, addresses, locations etc). It is important to keep identities safe (see O – Online Safety).
- Set privacy settings so that only people you trust can see your profile. Keep identities safe and encourage your child to keep full names, birthdates, addresses and personal information private.
- Encourage your child to only accept or add friends or contacts from other people that your child knows in person and trusts. If they are uncertain, suggest that they speak to you before accepting friendship from others online.
- Maintaining networks are as important as building them. It is important to encourage your child to nurture relationships and maintain positive connections online. It is also important to encourage your child to see the importance of the quality of their connections not just about the quantity of connections (ie the number of 'likes and followers').

Employment networking

Young people can network online to build connections and find employment opportunities. This can involve forming relationships online, sharing ideas, expanding knowledge, hearing about others' experiences or even joining professional groups or networking events. Networking can expand your professional circle and make meaningful connections for potential future employment opportunities.

Internet Matters, in their research into '*Children's Wellbeing in a Digital World*' (2024), found that the internet was a key source of inspiration to help children and young people with future careers. For example:

- 72% of children aged 9–16 perceived the internet as an important inspiration for future jobs.
- 74% of parents saw the internet as a tool to help children plan for the future.

There are a vast number of digital platforms highlighting potential companies for job-seeking children and young people. This includes not only networking sites like LinkedIn but also job boards, networking opportunities, mentoring and platforms that provide options to filter jobs based on specific criteria. This helps children and young people seek jobs based on their interests, experience and talents. Technology has also enabled children and young people to be entrepreneurs by setting up their own internet businesses, for example, selling items online or providing digital services.

LinkedIn is a key online platform used for professional networking and job opportunities and can be used to showcase your work experience and training (for over 16 year olds). Help your child draft a profile with a strong headline, detailing their skills and experience. You can also help them use social networking sites to promote their passion for specific industries and interests and build connections.

Make sure that your child is aware of their digital reputation and knows that social media profiles should show them in a positive light. Remind them that online activities, including social media posts, create a digital footprint that is visible to potential employers and can be permanent. Remember that potential employers often look at social media profiles on online activity when recruiting.

Practical TIPS

Practical tips on how to support children and young people on employment networking

- Young people will be more motivated and successful if they come up with their own online ideas and decisions themselves to help their employment journey. Help your child to pursue the career ideas that they are interested or passionate about and digital technology can help enable this. There are many online platforms that can help a young person explore their personality type, career options, ideas and make connections.

- You can also encourage your child to explore their interests by attending online networking events so as to connect with others. For example, online career fairs, workshops and webinars or conferences.
- Encourage young people to make connections where they feel confident and reaching out to others through platforms that they feel confident using. It can also help by contacting people they already know or know of.
- Identify online tools to help your child develop their CV or letters to potential employers.
- You can help your child to prepare questions to ask or preparing a digital 'pitch' which can include a summary of who you are, your experience, your skills, strengths and career aspirations.

Networking through online dating

There are endless dating apps and sites available for young people to meet others, make friends and build relationships. Online dating is a multi-million-pound global industry and gives young people the ability to connect with others 24/7. Ofcom (2023) has identified that 17% of 18 to 24 year olds use online dating services.

In the UK the legal framework surrounding use of dating apps by young people under 18 is shaped by a combination of age restrictions, child protection laws and online safety regulations. The Online Safety Act (2023) states that dating sites and other sites must implement robust age verification or age estimation methods to stop 'minors' accessing potentially harmful content. Whilst most dating sites require you to be over 18 years old and some will verify the age of their members, many will not and can be accessed using fake information. Each dating site will usually have membership criteria although sites will vary. There are various different niche sites and dating apps for adults, targeting those who are looking for friendships, romantic partners or those wanting to meet others with specific interests. However, dating sites specifically for young people are becoming more and more prevalent. For example, Our Teen Network, Teenber, Teenchat, Skout, Spotafriend and My LOL, to name but a few.

Whilst there are many positives for young people about online dating to connect and meet others, there are also risks. For example:

- **Online blackmail** happens when a child or young person is coaxed into sending nude or semi-nude photos over the internet with someone they have met on an online dating site. They are then blackmailed to make a financial payment to ensure that their photo will not be made public and posted online to their friends and family (see X – X-rated).
- **Catfishing** occurs when people create a false identity to lure a young person into a relationship (see C – Catfishing).
- **Online grooming** happens when someone forms a digital relationship with a child or young person. This can result in the child being manipulated into conducting sexual or illegal activities.
- Some dating apps often require people to make comments or rate images or photos, this can lead to **feelings of rejection, self-esteem and self-worth**.
- **Online sexual harassment** through social media, chat rooms or dating apps.

Practical TIPS

Practical tips to promote healthy relationships through online dating

Helping your child develop healthy and safe online relationships is key. Some of the tops tips for parents, carers and professionals include:

- Whilst it can sometimes be difficult to talk to your child about relationships, try to have an open conversation about the difference between healthy and unhealthy relationships.
- Discuss dangers and risks of online dating with your child – discuss the importance of 'really' knowing who you are speaking to and the importance of consent and consensual relationships.
- Encourage your child to set privacy settings so that only trusted people can see their profile. Encourage your child to keep their identify safe and keep full names, birthdates, addresses and personal information private.
- Help your child visualise a situation independent of their feelings and emotions by considering outcomes relating to different

choices that they could make. For example, thinking about 'what would happen if...?'

- Ensure your child is accessing age-appropriate sites to create their online relationships.

Activity – Giving your networks an MOT

Maintaining and nurturing networks are as important as building them. It is important to review your networks and determine where the gaps are.

Question	Yes	No
Does your social network make you feel positive and fulfilled?		
Does your social network support you to build social or employment connections?		
Are there gaps in your social networks?		
Does your social network challenge you in a positive and supportive way?		
Are the connections in your social network authentic and strong?		

If the answers are 'yes', it looks like your networks are working well. If you have answered 'no', you may need to review and enhance your networks using some of the practical tips above.

For further help and information

CEOP provides education, training, resources and information to parents and those working with children and young people. https://www.ceopeducation.co.uk/parents/articles/safer-online-dating-how-to-support-your-child/

Internet Matters provides advice and resources for parents. https://www.internetmatters.org/advice/by-activity/teens-and-online-dating-advice-hub-for-parents/teens-and-online-dating-advice-resources/

References

Department for Science, Innovation and Technology (2023) *Online Safety Act*. DSIT.

Internet Matters/BMG (2024) *Children's Wellbeing in a Digital World. Year Three Index Report 2024*. Internet Matters/BMG.

Ofcom (2023) *Online Nation*. Ofcom.

Ofcom (2023) *Understanding Online Communications Among Children: Quantitative research*. Ofcom.

O – Online safety

The chapter will cover:

- Online safety regulations and legislation highlights.
- An overview of research on online safety.
- Views of parents, carers and professionals.
- The different types of online harms.
- A trauma-informed approach to online safety.
- Practical tips and activities to promote online safety.

Online safety in a digital world

For many, the online world is a safe space to connect, learn and have fun, but for others it can be a source of harm which impacts on our mental wellbeing. Online safety refers to the precautions and practice that helps keep you and your child safe and protects them from harm when using digital devices or participating in any online activities. Risks that you and your child can witness include cyberbullying, phishing, identity, financial and security theft and scams, online grooming, and exploitation from others – to name but a few. It is important to be aware of online safety and actively promote open age-appropriate discussions with your child about potentially harmful situations that they could face online. As parents and professionals, we are responsible for helping to safeguard the wellbeing of our children online, and to ensure positive digital mental health.

Online safety regulations and legislation highlights

Ofcom's role is to ensure that online services are safer for the people who use them. They also make sure companies have effective systems in place to protect users from harm. Ofcom (2025) has set out rules on protecting children from harm online which states that tech companies will be legally required to block children's access to harmful content online under UK's Online Safety Act (2023) or face hefty fines. Social media and internet platforms will need to assess users' age to block access to harmful content, ensure harmful content is not recommended to children, remove content 'quickly' and provide clear reporting tools which are accessible to children.

Key research headlines on online safety

- Three in five children aged 13 to 17 have reported encountering potentially harmful content, over a four-week period.
- Three in every ten 8–12-year-olds who go online have seen something "worrying" or "nasty".
- The average age at which a child had first seen pornography is 13 years old (for those who have seen online pornography).
- Over half of 11- to 14-year-old boys were aware of and engaged with influencers.
- Over two thirds of children (9–17 years old) had experienced some form of online harm with girls being disproportionately exposed to certain harms in comparison to boys. For example, they are more likely to be bullied (13% compared to 7%), exposed to unrealistic body images (17% compared to 13%).

Parents and professionals play a key role in children and young people's online safety:

- The majority of parents (92%) are concerned about at least one online harm (Internet Matters, 2024).
- The majority of parents (90%) reported that they had spoken to their children about online safety (Ofcom, 2024).
- Children (85%) identify their parents as a primary source of information about online safety (Internet Matters, 2024).

- However, parents appear to underestimate their children's exposure to online harms despite an increase in becoming more concerned about what their children see online. For example, there has been a 22% increase in parents' concern about radical and extremist content and 15% increase in both suicide and self-harm content (Internet Matters, 2024).

Types of online harms

Children and young people can face several online harms in their digital world. For those who are already struggling with their mental health, exposure to online harms can have a hugely negative impact.

Figure 12: Types of online harms

Some of the examples of types of online harms highlighted by parents and professionals are highlighted below:

- **Phishing** – a type of scam where individuals or groups use digital communication to gain personal or sensitive information; for example, passwords, usernames, or financial details. There are different types of phishing attacks:
    1. **Email phishing** – attackers use email to communicate and to trick others to gain personal or sensitive information.
    2. **Smishing** – attackers use SMS or text to communicate and trick others to gain personal or sensitive information.

   3. **Vishing** – attackers use phone calls to communicate and trick others to gain personal or sensitive information.
   4. **Spear phishing** – attackers target a specific individual or group often through personalised communication.

- **Social media challenges** – a trend or activity that is performed and goes viral. These can be positive and fun (e.g. ice bucket challenge) but can also be dangerous, harmful and in some cases cause death (e.g. black out challenge – choking game, eating specific things – spices, drugs, laundry detergent).
- **Radicalisation and extremism** – can involve using online platforms to disseminate propaganda or ideologies and help recruit followers. Extremists can use social media to identify often vulnerable individuals exploiting their vulnerability and insecurities.
- **Sexual exploitation** – to be persuaded by others to share sexually explicit photos or videos or engage in sexually explicit conversations (see X – X-rated).
- **Scams and fraud** – including having their personal information stolen through identity theft, online scams which can lead them to sharing information or making payments (e.g. fake competitions or fraudulent websites), fake shopping sites, paying for fake in-game items, or romance scams through online scammers creating fake profiles to emotionally and financially exploit others.
- **Self-harm and suicide prevention** – in some cases social media can normalise self-harm and suicide which has the potential to increase risk, especially for vulnerable children and young people. This can include personal accounts, sharing tips, or online communities of those who are experiencing suicidal or self-harm thoughts (see U – Understanding digital self-harm).
- **Cyber bullying** – is persistent online harassment and intimidation which targets individuals, which could be through doxing, trolling or sending/sharing abusive messages and images.
- **Misinformation and disinformation** – misinformation is accidently sharing false and inaccurate information which perpetuates stereotypes and discrimination, whereas disinformation is sharing this information deliberately (see F – Fake News).
- **Gender-based harms** – include online domestic abuse (using technology for coercive and controlling behaviour), image-based sexual

abuse (non-consensual sharing of images and cyberflashing), online harassment or pile-ons (groups of co-ordinated individuals target a specific woman or girl online through threats, image-based abuse and misogynistic content) and misogyny (Ofcom 2025) (see M – Misogyny).

- **Hate speech** – which can include derogatory language, slurs or threats which discriminate against individuals or groups. It often spreads quickly through social media and the internet and can reach large audiences (see H – Online hate).

A trauma-informed approach to online safety

The impact of engaging in a trauma-informed approach in terms of children and young people's use of technology is imperative when considering online safety. The need to ensure that all tools, sites, platforms, apps and devices promote healing, support, empowerment, and prioritise emotional and psychological wellbeing. It is important to consider emotional safety to ensure digital content is appropriate and does not include any triggers which may retraumatise a child or young person.

Try to help children and young people use autonomy in their choice of digital activity but also set or co-design boundaries and digital routine with them. This can help establish stability, predictability and structure which is important in ensuring a trauma-informed approach to their wellbeing and to help build digital resilience.

Parents, carers and professionals' views on online safety

Online safety is a key area of concern for parents and professionals in terms of the worrying impact of online harms on children and young people's safety and mental health.

Professionals shared their concerns about the:

> *"unlimited space of unmonitored content, with little control of how to gage users real age, purpose of use and other protective factors";*

> *"Most of the children I work with are very unsafe online and there is a lot of cyberbullying".*

Another discussed parent's role in ensuring online safety:

> *"It is shocking how many parents cannot identify harmful content or realise that online or gaming communities are mature spaces where adults discuss mature content. Parents need to understand the platforms that children are using and know how to use it safely themselves. Not only can it be a bonding experience with their child to share in their interests, but parents can also learn alongside their child about the contents they are accessing and then have educational conversations about keeping safe online."*

Another professional reiterated the need to ensure an:

> *"open dialogue and explore together with kids. It is critical that young people can turn to a trusted adult if they see something harmful or get into trouble online...open and honest conversations need to be had."*

Parents and carers emphasised that their lack of digital skills and literacy impacts on their ability to support their children, and the lack of regulation were both key areas of online safety concerns. Several parents talked about the need for:

> *"tech organisations need to step up and take responsibility and improve regulation and monitoring".*

> *"It's like we are conducting an experiment with a whole generation of children. I am concerned by the lack of regulation and responsibility for any of us using some of these platforms".*

Other parents mentioned that:

> *"I need to educate myself about online safety to keep my child safe when using digital tech".*

> *"It's hard to better support a generation that is more knowledgeable than their parents around digital technology".*

It is also important to encourage supportive and positive interactions to ensure children feel safe, heard and understood through psychologically safe spaces. One parent talked about the need to:

> *"have open communication with them to ensure that they do not feel the need to hide anything from you. Create time and space to allow them to discuss things that are bothering them".*

> *"As parents, we need to provide opportunities so they (children) can talk to us, the good and the bad (from our perspective and theirs). If they know they will be reprimanded for engaging in certain aspects of technology, they are not going to speak to you when they get concerned themselves with it. And, let's face it, just because adults tell them not to engage in something does not guarantee that they won't engage in it, they will just hide their use from us".*

Practical TIPS: Practical tips for parents and carers to promote online safety

Practical tips can help parents and professionals to support their child to navigate online spaces more safely include:

- **Encourage open and honest conversations about online safety** by being curious and interested in children's online experiences by finding out what digital activities they enjoy but also their concerns. Encourage critical thinking, so that a child or young person can critically analyse what platforms or sites they are accessing and the impact that it has on them and their mental wellbeing. It is important to build and maintain environments to encourage children and young people to share with you their fears and experiences without judgement and with empathy.
- **Set boundaries** for positive online use so that children can make informed choices about their digital engagement. Age-appropriate boundaries and rules for devices and online use can be discussed together and co-produced with children and young people. As a child grows older and their digital skills and digital maturity changes so these can be reviewed.
- **Use safety features and settings** – whilst it can often remain difficult to keep up to date with the digital world, it is important to find out and discuss what devices, platforms and apps your children and young people are using and make sure that they have privacy and online safety settings set up. Some tips:
    - Use strong, unique and secure **passwords**. Change your passwords regularly and ensure that you don't use the same password for all platforms and devices. Some parental controls can even block passwords or settings being changed.
    - Keep **software up to date** to secure against hackers, predators or those seeking to exploit. Use reputable anti-virus software to protect against online scams or activity.
    - Protect and **safeguard personal information** and data and don't share passwords with others.
    - Use **reputable, authentic and secure websites**.

- **Try and limit apps and social media** accounts and delete those that are not in use or inappropriate.
- Use **parental controls** to help prevent access to inappropriate and harmful content, filter content, and manage screen time.
- **Monitor accounts** for unusual activity, block and report inappropriate activity or sites (see below).

Online safety activities

Supporting children and young people to remain safe online is essential. The following three activities can be used (check age-appropriate) to help improve online safety skills.

1. Five key online safety challenge

Work with your child/children to identify:

- Five things that I should do to make sure that I am safe online?
- Five things that I should never do to make me unsafe online?

Discuss what and why they have identified and the examples that they have given. This can be adapted according to the age of the child. For younger children get them to draw around both hands and use one hand to identify the positives and the other hand to identify the negatives.

Helpful hints of practical things that should be done and should never be done online are identified below:

Things that I should do to make sure that I am safe online.

- Change my password for all my devices regularly.
- Make sure my password is unique to me, not easily guessable and not share with anyone.
- Tell a trusted adult if I see anything online that upsets, frightens or worries me.
- Check my privacy settings regularly.
- Think before I share, post or like anything online.

Things that I should never do to make me feel unsafe online:

- Lend my devices to my friends or people that I don't know.
- Share my password with anyone.
- Use the same password for all my devices.
- Share any personal data or information with anyone.
- Ignore my privacy settings.
- Share private or explicitly images to anyone (they can often be misused or shared with others).

2. Stop, block and report quiz for 7 to 12 year olds

Read each message below and imagine you are chatting online.

Decide whether the message is SAFE or you should STOP and tell a trusted adult!

a. From Theo45 – "Hi! I'm Theo – I love Minecraft. Want to play too?"
b. RobloxFan5 – "Let's play Roblox. What's your name and address?"
c. Cutie5 – "You are really pretty. Prettier than your friends. Will you send me a photo?"
d. Friend456 – "I have a secret. I need to tell you my secret – want to know what it is?"
e. Evie2 – "This game is great. Want to play again?"

Encourage your child(ren) to make up some scenarios that they feel are safe.

Discuss with your child(ren) what is safe and what feels unsafe and the reasons for their answers. Encourage children to report anything to a trusted adult that feels wrong or unsafe – STOP, BLOCK and REPORT!

3. Periodic table of sinister emojis

Emojis are a popular and creative communication tool for children and young people. Most of the time emojis are used in a harmless way to express emotion, to replace or enhancing words or even just for fun. However, there can also be a more sinister and hidden way of using them, which link to online safety concerns (see S – Social Media for a breakdown of the use of emojis). For Working Parents has created a periodic table of sinister emojis to help parents and professionals understand the alternative meanings behind the more sinister emojis used.

How many of these emojis are you aware of?

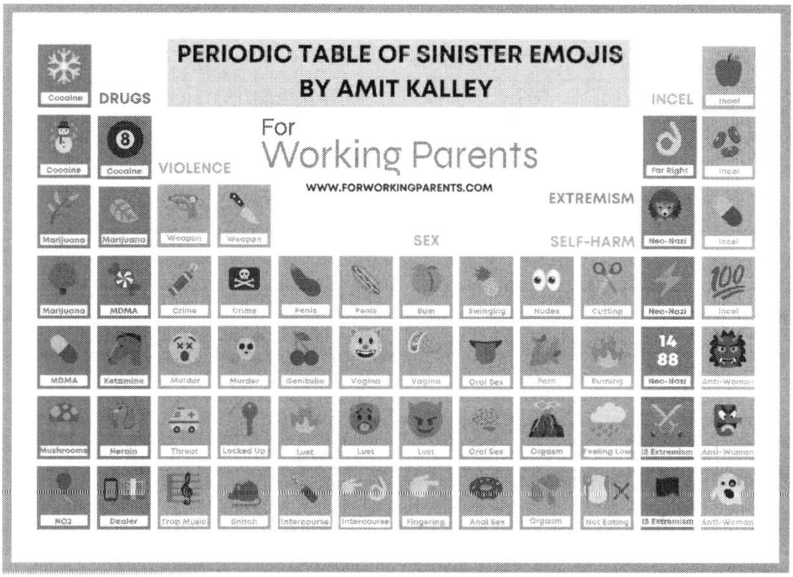

This resource is available to download and print in full colour online: **https://pavpub.com/mental-health/a-to-z-guide-to-children-and-young-peoples-digital-mental-health-resources**

For more information and advice on online safety

Online Safety

The NSPCC provide advice, information and helplines to support online safety: https://www.nspcc.org.uk/keeping-children-safe/online-safety/online-reporting/

Tackling online scams

https://www.internetmatters.org/resources/tackling-online-scams-guide/

Self-harm and suicide

Samaritans – https://www.samaritans.org/

Papyrus Prevention Young Suicide – https://www.papyrus-uk.org/

Additional support

Childline – https://www.childline.org.uk/info-advice/your-feelings/mental-health/suicide/ and https://www.childline.org.uk/info-advice/your-feelings/self-harm/

National Cyber Security Centre – if you receive emails that you are not sure about, forward it to report@phishing.gov.uk

Internet Watch Foundation – to report suspected sexual abuse online content: https://www.iwf.org.uk/en/uk-report/

Report Harmful Content – https://reportharmfulcontent.com/report/

References

Kalley, A. (2025) 'Periodic Table of Sinister Emojis'. www.forworkingparents.com

Internet Matters (2024) November Tracker. Internet Matters.

Ofcom (2024) *A Window into Young Children's Online Worlds*. Ofcom.

Ofcom (2025) *A Safer Life Online for Women and Girls: A Practical Guidance for Tech Companies*.

Ofcom (2025) 'Protecting children from harms online: Codes at a glance'. Ofcom.

Online challenges

https://www.fox10phoenix.com/news/dangerous-tiktok-challenges-list-kids-parents-march-2023

P – Parental controls

The chapter will cover:

- An overview of research on parental controls.
- Different types of parental control functions.
- Views of parents, carers and professionals on the use of parental controls.
- Practical tips and activities on the use of parental controls.

The role of parents

Parents and professionals have an important role in supporting their children online. There are various types of technical tools that you can use to monitor and limit the use of your children's digital devices including games, phones, computers and tablets.

Research on parental controls

Parents of older children are more likely to set rules for their children about being online. The *Children and Parents: Media Use and Attitudes* (Ofcom, 2024) found that parents were starting to engage rules about online use. Eight in ten parents of 16–17s (79%) have at least one rule about what their child does online, which had increased from 70% since the year before. The most common type of rule in place for this age group is around spending money online (52%) but also includes they types of website and apps they can use (32%).

Internet Matters research (2024) found that parents were more active in helping monitor and manage their children's online lives. They found that 21% of parents were managing their child's online use 'a lot'. They found that most parents (45%) were using parental controls or devices (e.g. manage what content they could access) and a third of parents looked at what their children were accessing online including apps, websites or games to ensure that they were suitable. Parents also noted that they removed devices if required (36%), and managed screentime by having clear rules about how much time they could spend online (38%).

It is important to review and adjust parental controls as children grow and become more mature and independent. The research (Internet Matters, 2024) states that whilst 29% of parents of 9–12 year olds manage their child's use a lot, this reduced to 16% for 13–14 year olds and 10% for 15–16 year olds.

Parental control functions

Parental controls have a range of functions and there are many apps or websites that can be set up on devices to help manage, monitor and limit usage. Some of the parental control functions can include, for example:

- **Monitoring activity** to identify what sites or online activity and apps your child is using.
- **Tracking the real-time location** of your child through digital locator devices or apps via a smartphone. Location tracking devices often use GPS to identify a person's location.
- Consider how to manage your child's **communication** by restricting who can communicate with them and who they can communicate with.
- **Restricting/blocking access** or filter content which may have inappropriate contents. Privacy restrictions and age-related restrictions can be put in place. This could include adult themes, drugs, violence, sex or other harmful contents.
- **Setting time limits** so that you can specify what time of day and for how long your child can go online for.

In terms of the ethics of using parental controls, it is important to consider both a balance of children and young people's privacy and their autonomy versus a parent's right to protect and ensure that they use devices safely.

It is really difficult for any parent to monitor all types of digital activity that their child is engaging in and virtually impossible to screen every call or message or constantly check website browsers but there are tools that can help provide support. There are a number of smart tools which help parents and professionals keep informed and set healthy boundaries, e.g. those which enable you manage app downloads, set screen time limits, view activity reports, restrict content, share location, block apps and manage screentime.

Parents, carers and professionals' views on parental controls

A large number of parents, carers and professionals identified the importance of parental controls as a tip to their peers to help children and young people's use of digital technology to support their mental health. Parents and carers focused on the need to set boundaries and monitoring and restricting the use of devices. They suggested:

"Get into the early habit of checking your children's use of technology so that it becomes an expectation".

"Put parental controls on, limit the time they spend on their phones and monitor groups chats".

"Set boundaries and stick to them! Agree times that they can use it and encourage them not to have multiple different social media profiles and platforms".

Another parent acknowledged the need of support to understand how to use parental controls:

"I struggle to work out which parental controls would be useful… it's a minefield of support out there but we are not the most tech savvy".

Teachers suggested the need to:

> *"have rigorous controls on what is downloaded and check phones regularly. Limit the amount of time allowed on their phones and model that yourself as a parent".*

> *"Introduce parental controls at an early age".*

> *"If technology is being used inappropriately limit use or increase monitoring.... parental controls are really important".*

Other professionals referred to:

> *"use of parental control functions and keeping a watchful eye over the content their children is accessing".*

> *"Monitor use, use parental restriction and follow guidelines".*

Practical TIPS – Practical tips on the effective use of parental controls

- Find out what parental controls are available, and which ones will be most suitable for your child dependent on ages and the devices used.
- Try to be transparent and fair, create an open dialogue with your child on the use of parental controls and the benefits of using them. If possible, ensure that clear agreements are jointly made about when, where and how parental controls are used.
- Help your child to set up their own digital boundaries through open conversations.
- Review and adjust parental controls as your child matures and demonstrates responsible online behaviour.

For further information and support on parental controls

Most platforms have parental controls tools which offer features for parents to monitor activity, online use and help set safe rules. Accessing parental controls including third party apps online can help you ensure that your child thrives safely online.

For additional support:

Internet Matters provides practical guides on how to set up parental controls on different platforms. https://www.internetmatters.org/parental-controls/

NSPCC provides advice on setting up parental controls. https://www.nspcc.org.uk/keeping-children-safe/online-safety/parental-controls/ and https://www.vodafone.co.uk/newscentre/smart-living/digital-parenting/digital-parenting-pro/

References

Ofcom (2024) *Children and Parents: Media Use and Attitudes*. Ofcom.

Internet Matters (2024) *Children's Wellbeing in a Digital World*. Internet Matters.

Q – Quality time

The chapter will cover:

- The benefits of offline quality time.
- Examples of alternatives to being online.
- The importance of living life for the moment.
- Views of parents, carers and professionals on the importance of being offline or reinforcing quality time when online?
- Practical tips and activities to enhance their quality time and encourage healthier digital habits and behaviours.

The value of no-tech time

Offline quality time is essential to positive mental wellbeing. For many of us, including children and young people, our digital use can be out of control. Too much time and reliance on our digital devices can impact our mood, relationships, behaviour and emotions. To maintain mental wellbeing it is important to encourage healthier online relationships and seek alternatives to screen time. Alternatives to screen time can often lead to healthier habits and a much more balanced lifestyle which can foster a range of skills including a sense of independence, social confidence, self-esteem and emotional resilience. The joy of missing out (see J – Joy of Missing Out) can have a positive impact on a child's quality of life by promoting personal wellbeing and contentment. The joy of missing out (JOMO) helps children value the positive outcomes of being away from their screens.

Examples of things to do away from screens

There are a number of meaningful things children and young people can do away from their screens.

- **Physical activity** – playing sports which promotes an active lifestyle, improved fitness, healthy growth, supports mental wellbeing and can teach a child how to work with others in a team towards a common goal.
- **Foster creativity** – drawing, painting, crafts, music, writing a poem or a story can all be ways to express thoughts and feelings and encourages imagination.
- **Learning** – reading books, learning how to cook or play a musical instrument can help develop practical skills.
- **Strengthen relationships** – meeting friends or joining a club can help build social and communication skills. It can help build social confidence and help reduce anxiety.

It is essential to have a balance between online digital activity and offline digital activity to ensure positive mental wellbeing. This is reinforced by a 12 year old girl who said:

"I realised I was feeling a bit grumpy and a bit lonely. I stopped seeing my friends after school and didn't do any of the after-school clubs they (my friends) were doing. Mum said I seemed sad and was spending too much time on my phone. I agreed to only use my phone after teatime. Now I have lots of time …. I now go to drama and dance class with my friends… before I was just at home on my phone".

What are the potential benefits of offline quality time?

- Reduce levels of stress – through a reduction in the stream of messages, information and notifications which lead to digital overload.

- Opportunity for taking part in more physical activity which can help keep bodies healthier and supports mental wellbeing.
- Help reconnect with nature and the environment by being present in the moment.
- More time to build social connections and interact with family and friends.
- Helps to improve sleep and concentration.
- More time for hobbies and creative and supporting activities.
- Less risk of exposure to online harms and cyberbullying.

Figure 13: Potential benefits of offline quality time

Living life for the moment

Living life in bite size-chunks through an online world reflects a cultural shift towards speed, constant stimulation and immediacy which ultimately affects the quality time of living life offline. The pressure of consuming information online in fast-paced and immediate bite-size chunks have implications to how we live our life. Quick digestible content through posts, memes, reels or carousels on social media that lacks depth and often context, can lead to often simplified understanding of information and affect the way in which we focus on concentrating. This constant stream of bite-size information can over-stimulate and lead to information fatigue. As a result, by living life through instant bite-size chunks our online world encourages us to live *for* the moment rather than appreciating quality time and living *in* the moment, being present and forming memories as opposed to constructing them as a post.

Parents, carers and professionals' views on the importance of being offline or reinforcing quality time when online

Parents and professionals recognised the importance of engaging in quality time when online or seeking offline activities as an alternative to being online. Many parents and professionals feed back on the importance of reducing screentime and promoting other activities to "*engage in family fun time*" or "*reduce screen time and replace with mood-boosting active past times*" and the need to "*help kids get off their screens and the mindless scrolling and connect with the "real world.*"

Many parents suggested digital breaks or complete digital detox as being a helpful tool to reinforce mental wellbeing. For example, one parent shared that they:

> *"went on holiday and decided to implement a digital detox for myself for 6 days. I was reluctant to switch off my phone, unsure of how I would communicate with my family and friends, how I could keep up to speed with my emails and take photos! I wasn't sure I had ever switched my phone off! The results were incredible… a sense of freedom, peace and lack of guilt for not responding to messages immediately. I was forced to be more present and explore alternative pursuits rather than filling up my time superficially scrolling on my screen. I read more, I connected with nature and spent more time with myself… yes, I will be doing this more regularly and hope to encourage the family to join me."*

Practical TIPS Practical tips to support children and young people to enhance quality time offline

There are a range of practical tips to support parents and professionals to improve quality time which encourage healthier online habits, for example:

- **Journal how much time is spent online** and how much time is spent doing activities that do not require digital technology.
- Allocating specific time to do **activities offline** including for example, reading a book, playing a game, riding a bike or baking a cake.
- Turn on '**Do not disturb**' notifications at certain times of the day and night.
- Revisit your **digital hygiene** – spring clean your apps including social media – remove those that make you feel inadequate, those you don't use or those you feel waste your time.
- **Parental controls** can be used to track and limit children's screen time (see P – Parental controls).
- A **digital detox**, **digital break** or planning unplugged hours can remove barriers that distract or deter us from living in the present and allows us to reconnect with the physical world and relationships by intentionally taking a break from any digital devices. Whilst it might be difficult to encourage a complete digital detox, why not encourage a digital break for periods of time, see what the impact is and discuss with your child the perceived benefits? You can detox digitally periodically, for example, certain times of the day, parts of the weekend or whilst on holiday. There are also various digital detox apps available to help reduce screen time, manage the use of digital technology and ultimately encourage healthier digital habits. These apps can help set limits and goals, block specific distractions, encourage screen breaks and set reminders, and promote digital online mindfulness. For children and young people there are some apps that help reduce screen time by gamifying the process and making it fun by incorporating rewards for achievements or streaks.
- Why not engage in a **family digital break?** Encourage a conversation about the benefits of healthier online usage and co-produce family goals and intentions.

Activity: A to Z game of digital alternatives

Encourage your children to identify all the things that they could do instead of engaging in digital activity beginning with a particular letter of the alphabet. One person starts the game by saying

"*I woke up today and rather th*an spending a lot of time on my phone, I did some colouring (A – Art).

The next person continues by saying "I woke up today and rather than spending a lot of time on my phone, I did some colouring (A – Art) and read a Book (B – book).

Continue around the group working through the alphabet, adding one more item to the end of the list each time. Here are some suggestions:

A arts and crafts
B bake a cake
C chilling in my room
D draw a picture
E do some exercise
F meet your friends
G play a board game
H play game of hide and seek
I ice some biscuits
J learn to juggle
K kick a football
L write a letter
M learn a musical instrument
N go on a nature walk
O organise your cupboards
P paint your nails
Q design a quiz
R read a book
S arrange a sleepover with friends
T arrange a day trip with the family

U play the ukelele
V plant some vegetables
W have a whistling competition
X arrange your own X factor talent show
Y try some yoga moves
Z go to the zoo

R – Racism

The chapter will cover:

- An overview of current research on online racism.
- The impact of online racism.
- How to spot racism online.
- Views of parents, carers and professionals on racism online.
- Practical tips and activities on how to prevent and tackle racism online.

When racism goes online

Racism happens when words or action are used to discriminate or disadvantage people because of their colour, race, nationality, culture or ethnic origins. Racism online can be overt through blatant and explicit racist hate speech or derogatory comments or covert which includes subtle or indirect microaggressions which are disguised through jokes, liking a comment or sharing a meme on social media. With the majority of children and young people spending more and more time online, the exposure to digital racism becomes a significant challenge.

All forms of racism can have extreme emotional and social impact on us all and we all have a responsibility to challenge it.

Research on racism online

The *Handbook of Children and Screens* (2025) focuses on online racism and its impact on children and young people of colour. It states that online racism can include virtual denigration, exclusion, abuse and dehumanisation based on race. It discusses how online racism can be subtle or explicit, interpersonal or structural but occurs through various forms including cyber bullying, misinformation and algorithmic bias. It also confirmed that the impact of exposure to online bullying for children and young people is poor mental health and academic outcomes.

Ofcom (2023) highlights that:

- Nearly a quarter of children 13–17 years old had encountered abuse or hate content online.
- 21% of children reported *"hateful, offensive or discriminatory content which targets a group or person, based on specific characteristics like race, religion, disability, sexuality or gender identity"*

Meanwhile, Internet Matters (2025) found that parents underestimate their children's exposure to online harms. For example: 17% of children reported that they had experienced hate speech online, but only 8% of parents stated that their children had been exposed to it.

What is the impact of online racism?

Online racism can have serious short-term and long-term impact on children and young people's social, emotional and academic lives.

- Online racism can have a fundamental impact on **mental health**. For anyone witnessing racist abuse online, it can lead to feelings of anxiety and depression which affect self-esteem, self-confidence and self-worth. For some children and young people, it may lead to isolation and loneliness as those who witness it may avoid engaging in online spaces through the fear of further abuse and feelings of being unsafe.
- Online racism can also affect a child's **academic performance** and educational experience. It may result in a child or young person withdrawing from academic activities and the learning environment fearing judgement or exclusion. The impact of online racism to a child's mental health can also impact on a child's ability to focus and perform academically, their motivation to learn (Springer, 2024) and potentially fear of attending school.

- The **social impact** of online racism can affect relationships, sense of identity and trust, and create feelings of isolation. Children and young people subjected to online racism can withdraw from social situations and relationships with others out of fear of being judged or excluded. This can exacerbate feelings of loneliness and social isolation which can potentially impact on a child's mental wellbeing. It can also lead to children and young people questioning their cultural and racial identity which can cause feelings of uncertainty and disconnection.

Racism can become normalised if children and young people have ongoing exposure; those subjected to it may become desensitised and see this type of behaviour and language as normal. Hence the need for parents and professionals to support children and young people to confront racist online behaviour and content.

How to spot racism online

Online racism and racial abuse can be both overt and covert and can take many forms, some of which are highlighted below:

- **Hate speech** – explicit slurs, threats or derogatory language (see H – Online hate).
- **Memes and images** – content which degrades cultures or different races.
- **Comments and likes** – responding in agreement or liking a derogatory comment, image or meme. These could include racial microaggressions which include unintentional comments that convey prejudice and discrimination.
- **Stereotyping** – content which perpetuates harmful racial stereotypes.
- **Misinformation** – false narratives that target specific cultures or races.
- **Online harassment** – abuse, including trolling or cyberbullying targeted at specific cultures or races.
- **Online exclusion** – excluding certain groups or cultures from online spaces.

Views of parents, carers and professionals on racism online

Feedback from a few teachers mentioned the impact of social media linking to pupil behaviour in the classroom. One teacher noted the increase in online racism but lack of skills to be able to challenge it:

> *"I am noticing a lot more of our students talking about discrimination online … it's the derogatory quips and comments …hidden comments that are simply racist! The thing is, it's hard to tackle it... don't want to get it wrong and offend anyone… hard to know what to do".*

Another teacher referred to:

> *"it is pupils' addiction to Tik Tok and Insta that is influencing such poor and disruptive behaviour in the classroom. It is the racist comments and memes that often mimic controversial social influencers viewpoints and propaganda".*

Practical TIPS Practical tips on how to prevent and tackle racism online

Parents, carers and professionals have a key role to help tackle online racism and create more inclusive online spaces in collaboration with children and young people. There are a number of practical ways to help which include:

- Have **open and honest conversations** with your child about racism, discuss historical and current events and historical figures and celebrities that impact on defining equality and inclusion and tackling racism. Keep these conversations regular and not just when it is in the news.
- **Monitor online spaces** to identify and address racist contents. If needed, use parental controls to help filter out harmful material.

- **Celebrate diversity** and different cultures to foster a sense of inclusion. Teach children about what racism is, how it manifests online and its impact.
- **Empower your child** to use social media responsibly, recognise racism on and offline and stand up against racism when they come across it.
- Encourage **critical thinking** to help your child analyse online content and recognise stereotypes, biases, online hate and misinformation.
- **Report online racism:**
  - A school or college will want to create safe and confidential spaces for pupils to report incidents. It is important for a school to address any reporting promptly.
  - Encourage your child to report any incidents of racism by knowing how and where to report it – through social media platforms or internet platforms.
- Seek **additional support** through a school or college or external organisations.

Activities

Three activities to tackle racism online and promote equality and inclusion include:

- Positive role models.
- Challenging racist words and language.
- History promotes equality and justice.

1. Positive role models

Encourage your child to identify positive influencers or celebrity and sports player role models who actively combat racism and promote equality.

- How do they stand up against racism?
- Find out about the impact that standing up to racism has had.
- Identify things that they could do to combat racism in similar way to the positive role models that they have identified.

2. Challenging racist words and language

Discuss the impact that words and images used online can have on the way you feel and behave. Racist words and language can result in feelings of poor self-worth and self-esteem, anger, anxiety and be traumatising. Help your child recognise the impact of racist words and language and the importance of replacing it with respectful and inclusive language.

Identify words or phrases that can challenge hurtful remarks. For example:

"We don't say word like that because they are unkind"

"It is not ok to say things like that"

"You are making me feel uncomfortable by saying that"

3. History promotes equality and justice

Exploring historical events or figures can be a powerful way for children and young people to understand and tackle racism in a positive way. Discuss the impact of historical racism and the link with modern day issues and racism.

- Find out and discuss with your child key times in history which inspired movements for equality and justice, e.g. abolition of slavery (1833); anti-apartheid struggles (20th Century); Windrush Generation (20th Century); or Civil Rights Movement (1950–60) or Black Lives Matter (21st Century).
- Identify key historical figures who championed equality and inclusion e.g. Nelson Mandela, Martin Luther King, Rosa Parks and Mahatma Gandi.

For more information and support on tackling online racism

Internet Matters provides information and resources on online hate. https://www.internetmatters.org/issues/online-hate/

NSPCC provides support for parents on how to talk to children about racism. https://www.nspcc.org.uk/keeping-children-safe/support-for-parents/children-race-racism-racial-bullying/

Stop Hate UK online hate resource hub.
https://www.stophateuk.org/resources/young-peoples-resource-hub/

Report a hate crime if a crime is committed against someone due to their disability, transgender identity, race, religion or belief or sexual orientation.
https://www.gov.uk/report-hate-crime

References

Ofcom (2023) *Online Experiences Tracker.* Wave 4, July 2023. https://www.ofcom.org.uk/media-use-and-attitudes/online-habits/internet-users-experience-of-harm-online

Ofcom (2023) 'Parents' rising concern over children online'. Ofcom.

Tynes, B.M., Willis, H.A., Maxie-Moreman, A., Ortiz, S.M. & English, D. (2025) 'Online Racism and Its Impact on Children, Adolescents, and Emerging Adults of Color.' In: D.A. Christakis and L. Hale (Eds) *Handbook of Children and Screens: Digital Media, Development and Well-Being from Birth Through Adolescence.* Springer, Cham. https://doi.org/10.1007/978-3-031-69362-5_39

S – Social media

The chapter will cover:

- Overview of the latest research on social media.
- Considering whether social media is a weapon or a tool.
- Assessing the benefits and risks to children and young people using social media.
- An exploration of the role of technology companies and social media.
- Parents, carers and professionals' views of social media.
- Practical tips and activities on how to support children and young people's responsible and safe use of social media.

Social media – ups, downs and role models

Children and young people use various social media platforms to stay connected with friends and family, for learning, networking, finding jobs and just for fun. For many young people, social media has a number of benefits including being able to interact and network with others, staying up to date with current trends and fashion, finding out information and sharing personal information and updates. However, for some children and young people social media is instrumental in having a negative impact on their mental wellbeing. Many of the negative impacts of social media for children and young people are covered within this Guide but of most concern is the exposure to online harms through social media including cyberbullying, online hate and inappropriate content.

At the same time, we have become used to seeing parents give their phones to children as a 'digital babysitter' so that their children are occupied whilst they complete their daily jobs or activities. At the same time, children and young people are used to seeing parents and professionals on their own phones, connecting with others through social media – so what role model are we presenting to our children, where the online world is part of their everyday lives?

Research on social media

Research indicates that children are actively using social media apps or sites, at a younger and younger age (Ofcom, 2025). Parents are recording that:

- Four in ten (37%) of children aged between 3 and 5 years old uses social media sites or apps.
- 36% of parents of children this age who use social media use it on their child's behalf.
- More than four in ten (42%) adults use social media sites alongside their preschool-age children.
- Two in ten (19%) preschool-age children use it independently (Ofcom 2025).

The *Children and Parents: Media and Attitude Report* (Ofcom, 2024) states:

- Three-quarters of social media users between the age of 8 and 17 have their own account or profile on at least one of the large social media platforms.
- Most social media platforms have a minimum age of 13, but six in every ten children aged between 8 and 12 years old have signed up with their own social media account.
- The majority of parents seemed unaware of the correct minimum age for social media platforms with only a third of parents (32%) correctly being aware that 13 years old is minimum age for most social media sites.
- One third of parents of 3- to 17-year-olds shared that they would be happy to allow their child to have a social media profile before they had reached the minimum age.

Both the benefits and disadvantages of children and young people's access to social media is highlighted in the same Ofcom Report (2024) which shows that:

- 68% of 8 to 17 year olds use social media, messaging or voice calling apps to help them feel closer to their friends.
- Two in five young people (40%) believe that people are "*mean and unkind to each other most or all of the time*".
- 87% state there is a need to "*feel popular*" on social media and messaging sites.

Is social media a weapon or a tool?

From speaking with parents, professionals and young people themselves there are some distinct benefits and challenges to using social media. The reality is that social media is clearly an integral part of children and young people's lives, and it is important to be aware of the ways it can be used as both a weapon and a tool. There is a need to educate and support children and young people to use it safely, responsibly and with the knowledge of its' limits and challenges and to ensure it is used as a tool rather than a weapon.

This image reflects an overview of the ways parents, professionals, children and young people describe social media as a both a weapon and a tool.

Tool	Weapon
Helps enhance **creative expression** by setting up and maintaining a social media profile.	The expectation to always be **digitally available** can lead to anxiety and the fear of missing out especially through 'streaks' and the number of likes received (see J – Joy of missing out).
Provides information and advice to help learn about **news** and increase awareness. It can also help children and young people better understand, extend or share what they are learning at school or college (see K – Keep learning).	Can provide **fake news, misinformation and disinformation** (see F – Fake news).

Tool	Weapon
Allows the building of **connections, social interaction and friendships** (see N – Networking).	Can result in exposure to **inappropriate and upsetting content, cyberbullying and online harassment which** can seriously effect children's mental health and wellbeing (see H –Online hate).
Builds **peer communities**, especially for those with similar interests, views and hobbies. Helps enhance feelings of belonging and identity.	Can enhance feelings of **inadequacy and insecurity** especially through comparison. For example, negative impact on perceived body image.
Builds **digital literacy and media skills** and positive digital footprint (see L – Literacy).	Can result in **poor digital footprint** and legacy (see L – Literacy).
Fosters digital **civic engagement** by giving children and young people a platform to access information, share their voice and hear other voices about key civic causes and campaigns, and meet others with similar interests.	Sedentary lifestyle and excessive use can affect **physical health** including sleep, weight gain (see W – Digital wellbeing).
Can help enhance feelings of **self-esteem and self-worth** by receiving positive feedback and interaction with others.	Can enhance feelings of **poor self-esteem and self-worth** by receiving negative feedback through interaction with others.
Provides **positive information and support** on mental wellbeing by offering counselling, advice and signpost to organisations.	Can be a **time sponge** – wasting time through excessive use and scrolling and can lead to missing out of other activities (see Z – Zoning out).
Offers **fun and entertainment** from playing games or doing puzzles, listening to music or watching funny videos.	Can result in exposure **to online hate, hate speech, violence and discrimination** including misogyny and racism (see R – Racism, M – Misogyny and H – Online hate)

The role of technology companies and social media

We all have different perceptions of whether or not children and young people should use social media, what age they should access it and which platforms are most suitable or unsuitable. However, the law states that the age limit for social media use in the UK is 13 years old. The Online Safety Act (2023) states that tech companies must protect children and young people from harmful content which includes enforcing age limits and assessing risk to children. Ofcom's role is to act as the independent regulator and ensure that the act is enforced, and technology companies adhere to the legal obligations.

We know that the world of social media is an international multi-billion pound phenomena, and technology companies play the ultimate role in shaping how the platforms work and how we engage with and experience them. They set rules about what is included or not included and use algorithms to enhance targeted digital use. They also collect data on our personal social media use, interests and behaviour online. However, research (Ofcom, 2024) suggests that 22% of eight to seventeen year olds lie about whether they are 18 or over on social media apps. By lying about their age, children and young people are more likely to be exposed to online harms. Whilst we question whether technology companies are doing enough to protect children and young people online, the implementation of the Online Safety Act (2023) from July 2025 requires tech companies to ensure highly effective age verification and assurance.

There is an increasing call from some parents and professional bodies for a total social media ban for children under the age of 16. This links to a push towards the need to protect children and young people from online harms. Across the world, several countries ban or restrict access to social media. For example, Australia has recently approved a law which bans children under the age of 16 from creating or maintaining accounts on social media platforms.

Parents, carers and professionals' views about social media

Parents mostly noted the negative aspects of social media including the excessive time spent and risks of bullying online through social media platforms. Professionals were in agreement with the same negative factors but many also highlighted the risks around online safeguarding. One practitioner noted that:

> *"young people are very reliant on all the platforms, social media never stops. It is an addiction and a pandemic in its own right".*

A teacher recognised the positive opportunities of using social media, but counterbalanced this with some of the challenges for children and young people by stating:

> *"I believe that there are benefits to social media that can give young people opportunities to connect with and understand others…broaden their views by having access to a network of diverse cultures and beliefs. There is, however, the danger of being exposed to harmful content and people… cyberbulling. Without information on how to stay safe online and poor media literacy and critical thinking, young people can become very vulnerable by using social media".*

One parent of a 14 year old daughter identified a tip for other parents on how to take a digital break:

> *"When (my daughter) asked me if she could download X (a social media platform) because all her friends had it, I reluctantly agreed on the proviso that I would download it too. Three months later we discussed the benefits of it. She agreed it was exhausting trying to keep up with the hundreds of snaps she got – hundreds a day. She said it made her feel anxious when she didn't respond to all the messages and straightaway. We both agreed to take a break ... and she hasn't mentioned or asked to re-download the app".*

Practical TIPS: Practical tips on how to support children and young people's responsible and safe use of social media

Supporting children and young people on social media can be challenging but there are some practical ways in which to help children and young people create a supportive and safe online environment.

- **Keep conversations open** – Create safe spaces for your child to share their online experiences without judgement.
- **Keep up to date** – Familiarise yourself with the social media apps your child uses by asking them what they use and why.
- **Set boundaries** – Work with your child to establish and review age-appropriate rules on screen-time, appropriate apps and platforms, and netiquette.
- **Take a break** – Encourage your child to keep taking breaks and seek a balance in offline healthy activities.
- **Keep safe** – Talk with your child about the risks of sharing personal information, interacting with strangers and online harmful content. Consider using age-appropriate parental controls.
- **Set an example** – Children often mimic the behaviour of their parents so set an example in your use of social media.
- **Mood check** – Encourage your child to check how they are feeling before they go online. Will social media make them feel better or worse?
- **Digital footprint** – Your digital footprint is relatively permanent and can affect online and offline reputations. Encourage your child to look for their social media digital profile through a search engine by typing their name or review their social media profiles. Is this the image they want to portray to others, including future employers? If not, contact websites or platforms and get them to remove it, revisit social media privacy settings so that only those people they know and trust have access; delete accounts and platforms that they do not use them anymore; and help them create a positive digital footprint.

Activities

These activities have been designed to test parents' and professionals' social media digital literacy skills. Enjoy doing these quizzes with teenagers (some are not appropriate for young children due to content).

1. Conversation starters to help you and your child talk about social media
2. Social media quiz
3. Social media acronyms quiz
4. Social media numeronyms quiz
5. Social media slang quiz

1. Conversation Starters To Help You And Your Child Talk About Social Media

For many parents, carers and professionals, it can be daunting to talk about social media to your child. Open conversations can help build relationships and trust with children and young people, so be curious and interested to find out more about what platforms they use, why they use it and how it impacts on their feelings. The activity below provides conversation starters to help you talk to your child about social media.

'Conversation starters' to help you and your child talk about social media

Here are some conversation starters to help initiate a discussion about social media with your child:

- What apps and websites do you like to use and why?
- What types of social media do your friends use and why?
- What are the best things about using social media? (e.g. connecting with friends, finding out information, relaxing, stops boredom)
- What are the worst things about using social media? (e.g. wastes time, makes be cross, comparing myself to everyone who is perfect or lives a perfect life)

- Have you tried to cut down? How much time you spend on social media and why?
- How could you try and cut down on the time you spend on social media?
- How do social influencers make their money? What do you think about people that make their money as a social influencer?
- Do you think social media affects how you and your friends are feeling and their mental health?
- How could adults use social media better? What social media do you think adults are missing out on?

2. Social media quiz

Social media are platforms and applications that enable users to create, share and interact with each other. Children and young people often know how to use them to post texts, images and videos, find out information, meet new friends and play games.

Whilst many apps are used harmlessly by children, it is important to be aware of the dangers of some of the apps and ensure that you speak with your child about what and how they use these apps. For example, some apps have location-sharing features which can be used inappropriately, share adult and harmful content, are less moderated and use anonymous messaging which can lead to interaction with strangers and grooming, or promote perfect body ideals. Social media apps come and go, reflecting the changing interests and digital trends of young people.

Keep being curious and discuss with your child:

- Discuss with your child which apps they use and why they use them.
- What other apps does your child use and why do they use them?

There are a huge range of online platforms and apps. How many did you recognise? Here are the names and roles of a selection of them:

Netflix Subscription based streaming tv and movies	**Instagram** Visual platform-sharing photos and reels	**Tik Tok** Used to create & share long and short form videos, memes
Roblox Online game platform which allows in-game chat	**WhatsApp** Cross platform messaging app for groups or peer to peer	**Snapchat** Mobile messaging app
BeReal Allows sharing of real life unedified photos of daily life	**Twitch** Livestream platform for gaming and creativity	**Yubo** Social discovery app for teens to meet new people and livestream
Reddit Social news forum and platform for discussion	**YouTube Kids** Video app & website for children	**Discord** Chatrooms connecting friends through voice, video and chat
X (Twitter) Microblogging and social networking	**Pinterest** Visual discovery platform with focus on creative content	**Telegram** Encrypted messaging platform

3. Social media acronyms quiz

Children and young people use acronyms in social media for speed as typing out full words takes time, and to help them fit into their peer groups. For some it can be for secrecy and privacy and for others it is just for fun. Many of these acronyms have different meanings for different children and young people but the most popular definitions are included below.

Why not see if you are aware of the meanings behind these social media abbreviations? Are there any others you are aware of?

How many social media abbreviations do you know?

BF	Best friend or boyfriend
FOMO	Fear of missing out
IDK	I don't know
smash	I would have sex with you or hot/attractive
srs	serious
PDA	Public display of affection
ROFL	Rolling on the floor laughing
NSFW	Not safe for work (something that should not be shown in public
BRB	Be right back
WTPA	Where is the party? ('Where the party at?')
OOMF	One of my followers (secret way to talk to followers)
MYOB	Mind your own business
PIR	Parent in room
POS	Parent over the shoulder (warning a parent is watching)
PAW	Parents are watching
BAE	Baby (girlfriend or boyfriend) or before anyone else
FWB	Friends with benefits
TDTM	Talk dirty to me
IRL	In real life
LMIRL	Let's meet in real life

SEGGS	Sex
Lit	Exciting or amazing
Cap	Fake or lie
Basic	Boring or average
Skl	school
CTN	Can't talk now
AFK	Away from the keyboard
Slay	Doing something well or that's cool
ILY	I love you
IWSN	I want sex now
KPC	Keeping parents clueless
WTTP	Want to trade pictures/photos
MGTOW	Men going their own way
PUA	Pick up artist – men or boys who use manipulation to attract and seduce others
GNOC	Get naked on camera

4. Social media numeronyms quiz

Some numeronyms are used in social media. Numeronyms are words partly or completely made up of numbers. Many of these acronyms have different meanings for different children and young people but the most popular definitions are included below.

How many numeronyms are you aware of?

P999	Parent alert
53X	sex
F2P	Free to play (often used in gaming)
L8R	Later
477	Best friends for ever
70	I'm sad
CU46	See you later for sex
8	Oral sex
182	I hate you`
1174	Party
143	I love you
601	Happy birthday
LH6	Let's have sex
910	Sorry I hurt you
G2G	Got to go
420	Marijuana
CD9	Parent alert
9	Parent watching
99	Parent gone
404	Don't have a clue
41	Call me
46	Hug
121	I need to talk to you
607	I miss you

5. Social media slang quiz

Here is a list of words, many used by children and young people on social media platforms. Check your understanding of the meaning of the words below (see Glossary for correct definitions)

Doxing	Roasting	Blog
Cyber flashing	Meme	Catfishing
Baiting	Phishing	Likes
Phubbing	Griefing	Fraping
Skin gambling	Doom scroll	Outing
Troll	Bit coin	Flaming

References

Online Safety Act (2023)

Ofcom (2024) *A Window into Young Children's Online Worlds*. Ofcom.

Ofcom (2024) *Children's Online User Ages*. Ofcom.

Ofcom (2024) *Children and Parents: Media Use and Attitudes Report*. Ofcom.

Ofcom (2025) *Children and Parents: Media Use and Attitudes Report*. Ofcom.

Online Safety Amendment (Social Media Minimum Age) Act 2024

T – Trolling

The chapter will cover:

- An overview of research and laws on trolling.
- An outline of some of the different types of trolls.
- Reasons why people may troll and some of the effects of trolling.
- Practical tips to support children and young people to tackle trolling.

What is trolling?

The word 'trolling' is linked to the fishing term meaning that a person (a troll) attaches their bait (comment) and waits for others to bite (react or provide a response). Trolling happens when someone posts or comments online to deliberately provoke a reaction or response. A 'troll' will often make comments that are deliberate and controversial with the aim of starting an argument or causing upset. These posts often include aggressive, cruel, embarrassing and hateful comments which can have huge psychological and behavioural impact. Trolling can happen on video streaming sites, video games, on social networks, online forums, message boards, chat rooms or even as personal emails. Internet trolling is a well-documented issue raised by a number of high-profile celebrities who have shared their experiences of being trolled and the huge impact that it has had on them.

Research and laws on trolling

The *Online Experiences Tracker* (Ofcom Online Nation Report, 2024) states that:

- 69% of young people aged 13–17 and 80% of 18–24 year olds have encountered potentially harmful content online.
- The most common potential harms that 13–17 year olds encounter include offensive or 'bad' language (35%); misinformation (33%); and trolling (21%).
- 23% of girls aged 13–17 years olds recorded experiencing trolling online in comparison to 18% of boys of the same age.

Despite a high number of young people experiencing potentially harmful online content the research shows that teenagers were less likely to report that they had experienced potential harm in comparison to adults. Ofcom (2022) identified that the main reason for young people not reporting online harm was that:

- They didn't see the need to do anything (29%).
- 21% didn't think it would make a difference.
- 12% were not sure where to report it or who to inform.

Online trolling is different to cyberbullying (see O – Online safety). Whilst trolling is about people posting comments to ultimately get a reaction or response from a wide audience, cyberbullying is online abuse and targets a specific individual. There are various laws which make trolling illegal in Britain if it includes threats of violence, hate speech (see H – Online hate), harassment and/or stalking. For example, the Communications Act (2003) states that sending grossly offensive messages, or messages of an indecent, obscene or menacing character is an offence. The Malicious Communication Act (1988) states it is illegal to cause distress or harm to another person through electronic communication. The Online Safety Act (2023) refers to trolling-related behaviour under the broader regulation of harmful, abusive or illegal online content. The enactment of this Act more recently has stated that tech companies have a legal duty to assess the risks of trolling-related harm and prevent and remove harmful abusive content.

Different types of trolls

There are various different types of trolls, who can be categorised into different types depending on their intent, audience and the way in which they wish to incite a reaction. Some of the different types of trolls include, for example:

- **Celebrity focused trolls** – those who seek attention by provoking celebrities online.
- **Gaming trolls** – provoke a reaction by disrupting game play for others. This can include abusive voice chat or 'griefing'.
- **Flame trolls** – who provoke a reaction with offensive inflammatory remarks online.
- **Grenade trolls** – who incite a reaction by throwing an abusive or shocking comment into an online discussion and then disappearing and not commenting again.
- **R.I.P. trolls** – who provoke reactions by targeting memorial sites or online tributes.
- **Group trolls** – this includes a number of people who work together to provoke a reaction by spreading misinformation or manipulating online discussions.

Why do people troll?

There are many reasons why people troll and each troll will have different reasons for doing so: boredom; malice; jealousy; to create disruption, or to seek attention; others will troll 'for fun'. Most of all, a troll's main aim is to provoke emotional reactions from other people. Whilst trolls could be someone your child knows, more often than not trolls are anonymous and use made-up profiles and pictures with unidentifiable usernames.

Helpful hint: Remind your child that most trolls look for a response or a reaction. It is important to encourage them not to engage in a response with a troll, however tempting it is to react – a lack of reaction is a troll's worst nightmare!

What is the effect of trolling?

Trolling can often affect the mental wellbeing of those children and young people who witness it. As well as a negative psychological, trolling can also have a physical impact, for example:

- **Psychological impact** which could result in low self-esteem and self-worth as well as contributing to emotional distress, anxiety and depression.
- **Behavioural impact** on children and young people can include substance misuse, withdrawal from social life and social isolation, detrimental impacts on personal relationships and, in some (extreme cases), self-harm and suicide ideation. (Department for Digital Culture and Media, 2018).

Practical TIPS

Practical tips on supporting children and young people to tackle trolling

Trolling can affect your child's emotional and physical wellbeing, so it is important to understand why and how trolls operate online. Here are some practical tips to help deal with trolling:

- **Talk regularly and openly** about trolling to your child, explaining what it is and making sure they feel confident that they can seek a trusted adult to talk to if they are worried about trolling online.
- Try to **resist the urge to respond** to hateful messages as this can often make things worse as trolls are often seeking reactions from those they are trolling. It might be really tempting to respond, but a lack of reaction to the troll is best.
- Take a **screenshot** or record any nasty messages, recordings and URLs – this could provide evidence if things escalate and you need report any trolling activity.
- Set up **parental controls** and **block** anyone causing harm and report hateful messages through platform reporting tools.
- Support your child to **report** any trolling activity.
- Encourage your child to **stop and think** before posting anything online and to think of the reactions and impact that posts will have on those who receive them.
- Encourage children to **seek help and support** by talking to a trusted adult (like a parent or teacher) or accessing support groups.

For further information and support

The **Child Exploitation and Online Protection** (CEOP) provides up to date information and advice on how to report online abuse. www.ceopeducation.co.uk

Childline provides help and advice call 0800 1111 or for www.childline.org.uk

UK Safer Internet Centre offers advice on how to use the internet safely www.saferinternet.org.uk

References

Department for Digital, Culture, Media and Sport/Centre for Strategy and Evaluation Services (2018) *Rapid Evidence Assessment: The Prevalence and Impact of Online Trolling*. DfDCMS/Centre for Strategy and Evaluation Servcies.

https://assets.publishing.service.gov.uk/government/uploads/system/uploads/attachment_data/file/973971/DCMS_REA_Online_trolling__V2.pdf

Ofcom (2024) *Online Experiences Tracker*. Ofcom.

Ofcom (2024) *Online Nation 2024 Report*. Ofcom.

Ofcom (2022) *Online Nation 2022 Report*. Ofcom.

Malicious Communication Act (1988)

Communication Act (2003)

Online Safety Act (2023)

U – Understanding digital self-harm

The chapter will cover:

- An outline of what is meant by the term 'digital self-harm'.
- An overview of research on digital self-harm.
- Why does digital self-harm happen?
- Views from young people on digital self-harm.
- Views of parents, carers and professionals on digital self-harm.
- Practical tips and activities to helps to tackle digital self-harm.

What is digital self-harm?

Digital self-harm is seen as a form of cyber-bullying where the victim and the perpetrator are the same person. Digital self-harm refers to posting hurtful, negative or abusive things about yourself of social media or gaming platforms. This is a form of self-bullying and, for many, the posts, images and blogs are made anonymously or using a fake name.

Research on digital self-harm

Whilst there is limited research and data available on digital self-harm, there is research (Patchin, 2024) that shows that there has been an increase with 9–12% of young people researched in USA had participated in a form of digital self-harm.

The research identified that LGBTQ+ young people were 2.5x more likely to take part in digital self-harm. What is more, those who have experienced cyberbullying themselves were seen as more likely digitally self-harm.

Why does digital self-harm happen?

There are many reasons why children and young people may engage in digital self-harm which will vary according to an individual, but examples of reasons could include:

- To pre-empt and control negative comments or criticism.
- Seeking validation and reassurance after receiving negative messages online.
- Expressing emotional distress, sadness or unhappiness.

Young people's views of digital self-harm

Some of the young people consulted raised digital self-harm as an issue (Randell, 2024). They talked about themselves or their friends using social media to make comments about themselves, hoping that others disagreed. They talked about putting comments online such as *"I am fat"*, *"I am ugly"*, *"I have got no friends"*, *"I hate myself"* – often this resulted in others disputing these comments and offering positive comments instead. However, there is a danger in making self-loathing comments online, which can result in others confirming statements and therefore reinforcing negative feelings and affecting mental health and wellbeing.

Parents, carers and professionals' views on digital self-harm

Feedback from some parents and professionals identified their concerns about self-harm in general but only a minority raised digital self-harm. One practitioner said

> *"I have seen a large increase in self-imposed exclusion where young people are confined to their rooms engaging with friends exclusively online. However, I have seen how this isolation can cause considerable impact on young people's mental health. I have also supported young people who engage in online point-scoring games where they get points for harming themselves".*

A parent shared their concerns about how

> *"there is no monitoring about the content posted, seen or shared online. I know my child is depressed and says awful things about herself so that others respond more positively, but sometimes they don't reply, or they agree with her, reinforcing the negative comments and then it just makes her feel worse".*

Practical TIPS Practical tips on preventing digital self-harm

There are various practical ways to support and prevent digital self-harm, including:

- **Keep talking** and encourage open conversations with your child to discuss digital pressures and emotional challenges.
- **Promote your child's self-worth** by acknowledging and encouraging their strengths and validate their emotions by making sure that they are listened to and heard.
- **Encourage a balance** between screen time and activities offline.
- Encourage your child to develop a **tracker** to help track emotions, triggers and self-harm urges but use the tracker to identify strategies to distract from feelings and urges to self-harm
- Support your child to seek **professional support** if needed.

Activities

There are a number of activities that can help support resilience and emotional wellbeing.

1. Create a digital happy box.
2. Relaxing body scan.
3. Positive affirmation cards.

1. Create a digital happy box

Why not encourage your child to create a personalised 'digital happy box' which can help provide distractions, offer inspiration and ways in which to relax. Whilst there are virtual hope or happy box apps available, we suggest creating your own which could include, for example:

- Positive messages from friends or family.
- Images that make you smile.
- Screenshots of positive affirmations.
- Download meditation apps to help you relax.
- Puzzles or quizzes.
- Download some podcasts.
- Download your favourite music.
- Photos of things that make you happy – pets, or a special place or memory.

2. Relaxing body scan

A body scan for your or your child can help you relax, unwind and let go. Why not encourage body scanning before bedtime. Make sure your child is comfortable, warm with no other noises to distract them.

- Let yourself be still and quiet.
- Take three really deep and long breaths.
- Start with toes and feet, then legs, tummy, arms and hands, shoulders, neck and face. Encourage relaxion, soft breathing with calmness and letting go of all tension, allowing each area to be relaxed and heavy.
- Finish by helping your child picture their whole body feeling calm and relaxed.
- Take several breaths and repeat.

3. Positive Affirmation Cards

Why not collect or create your own unique affirmation cards for yourself or encourage your child to make them. They are a positive tool to help instil resilience, positivity, happiness and confidence. Affirmation cards can be printed out and displayed next to your bed, in the car, in packed lunch boxes, on the bathroom mirror or on the back of doors as a reminder to create positivity which encourages self-belief and self-worth.

- I am a good friend.
- I am confident.
- I believe in myself.
- I am resilient.
- I am loved.
- I can get through anything.
- I am perfect just the way I am.
- I am free to be myself.
- I am beautiful inside and out.

For more information and advice

Samaritans offer someone to talk to 24 hours a day, everyday support: samaritans.org/how-we-can-help/contact-samaritan/

Childline offers information and advice: childcare.org.uk

Internet Matters provide information and advice on dealing with self-harm: internetmatters.org/issues/self-harm/dealing-with-self-harm/

If you are really worried about your child, seek professional support.

References

Patchin, J.W. & Hinduja, S. (2024) 'Adolescent digital self-harm over time: prevalence and perspectives, Journal of School Violence, 1–13.

V – Vlogging

The chapter will cover:

- An overview of research on vlogging.
- The difference between vlogging, blogging and live streaming.
- Benefits and negatives aspects of blogging.
- Views of parents, carers and professionals on vlogging.
- Practical tips and activities to promote safe and responsible engagement with vlogging.

What is vlogging?

Vlogging is a very popular way for children and young people to share their lives, opinions and talent with the online world using social media platforms. A vlog is pre-recorded video content that is shared on video sharing platforms (e.g. Tik Tok, YouTube or Instagram). More and more young people are not just watching vlogs but also vlogging themselves. Vlogging topics range from gaming, lifestyle (cooking, fashion, make-up), travelling and gaming to physical and mental health. The global vlogging industry is a huge part of the digital economy where vloggers can capitalise on turning their digital content into vast incomes through revenue generated from paid advertisements, merchandise or even sponsorship.

Research on vlogging

Video sharing platforms (VSP) such as YouTube, Tik Tok and Twitch are increasingly popular amongst children and young people. Ofcom (2025) identified that over two-thirds (66%) of 3–17-year-olds had watched live-stream videos, an increase from 2022 (58%), a rise which is specifically driven by 8-12-year-olds.

YouTube remains the most popular VSP with over 2.85 billion users globally (Global Media Insight, 2025), although Tik Tok and Snapchat are also influential platforms used by children and young people. Ofcom's *Media Nations Report* (2024) reported that video sharing platforms accounted for 40% of 4–15-year olds' total in-home video time; 16–24-year-olds were spending on average of 1 hour and 33 minutes a day using VSP as part of their in-home video time.

There is a growing interest in young people livestreaming their own videos as the access to technology has made it easier to livestream anytime and from anywhere, and young people use social media platforms that allow them to express themselves creatively. Ofcom (2025) found that 16% of 3–17-year-olds livestream their own videos.

The difference between a vlog, a blog and live streaming

Bloggers, vloggers, live streamers and social influencers all play a key part in shaping children and young people's digital culture through their different online perspective and content, all of whom target their audience's interests. They all use different digital media to share their thoughts, ideas, activities and beliefs. Many social influencers use vlogging and blogging to engage their audience. Influencers often use social media platforms to influence the way their audience thinks and their purchasing choices, often receiving payment or free products for doing so (see I – Influencer). The differences between vlogging, blogging and live streaming are:

- **Vlogging (video blogging)** is pre-recorded video content loaded onto the internet, often through video sharing platforms to share experiences, personal opinions and knowledge online to connect with their audience. Vlogs are pre-recorded and can be edited. Many high earning vloggers have a huge and loyal following. Vlogging is one of the most favoured forms of online content creation today with millions of views across a range of digital platforms.

- **Blogging** (web log) is sharing written articles or posts (blog) online.
- **Live streaming** is the broadcasting of live videos on the internet (e.g. events, daily life or games) through video sharing platforms. Live streaming content cannot be edited.

The benefits and challenges of vlogging

The upsides

The are many reasons that children and young people engage in vlogging (and blogging) themselves, for example:

- Many children create vlogs themselves to **seek fame and recognition**. Livestreaming can bring instant visibility. For many young people, vlogging is a way of creating their own 'personal brand' to share their talents, messages and interests.
- There can be a **financial gain** (for example, through sponsorship and brand deals, the numbers of likes, comments or views, or by selling merchandise).
- It can help young people **express themselves** freely and creatively, for many in a way that they find difficult to do face to face.
- It can help young people **enhance their digital literacy skills** by learning how to create digital material and navigate digital platforms.
- It can also help **build self-confidence and self-worth** by encouraging young people to express their thoughts and feelings online. Comments and likes from others can provide immediate feedback and validation which for many is psychologically rewarding.
- It helps **build digital communities** for young people to interact with other like-minded people with similar interests.

The downsides

Whilst there are a number of benefits to engaging in vlogging, there are also **negative aspects to vlogging**, including for example:

- Remaining **safe online** through the loss of privacy if personal information is shared and, in some circumstances, this could lead to cyber bullying and online harassment.

- Being subject to negative comments and feedback can affect children and young people's **feelings of self-esteem and self-worth** which ultimately impacts their mental wellbeing.
- A constant need for **personal validation** through likes and views can lead to an unhealthy dependence on vlogging and social media.
- Curated online personas and the constant need to be 'perfect' which may not be real can lead to **unrealistic expectations** on friendships, mental wellbeing and life in general.

Parents, carers and professionals' views on vlogging

Whilst one parent noted the positive aspects of vlogging, others articulated their concerns about the type of vlogging content their children were accessing. A parent shared that:

> *"my daughter loves GRWM (get ready with me) videos. She says it's a great way of learning lots of new stuff – make up and what to wear …how to do her hair. She finds it kind of …relaxing, like getting ready to go out with her best friend".*

However, other parents outlined their concerns:

> *"It worries me that these vloggers are employed to promote expensive products which my kids spend their money on".*

> *"Some of these vloggers promote fake and perfect looking lives and it makes kids feel inadequate".*

Practical TIPS Practical tips on supporting children and young people's safe and responsible engagement with vlogging

There are a number of ways in which to support children and young people who engage with vlogging which include:

- **Talk with your child openly** about the benefits and risks of livestreaming and help them spot the digital 'red flags' of cyberbullying, trolling and online grooming.
- Make sure you and your child understand the **specific guidelines and rules** on content, age restrictions and safety measures on each video sharing platform that they use.
- Make sure **privacy settings** are set up to control who can and cannot access vlog or blog content.
- Encourage children and young people to be **mindful of the content** that they create and view in terms of the negative impact of the messages and content shared. Help them to think before they share anything online.
- Discuss with your child what and why they want to vlog or blog – the messages, the audience and **impact of the content** creation on themselves and others. Watch and look at vlogs/blogs together and discuss what is okay to share and what to do if something feels 'off'.

Activities to promote positive vlogging

1. Conversation starters to promote positive vlogging activity.
2. Create your own family vlog.

1. Vlogging conversation starters aimed at children who are vlogging or considering vlogging?

Having an open and honest conversation with your child about the benefits and risks of vlogging is important. Show genuine interest without starting with criticism! Conversation starters can include:

- What do you like about livestreaming?
- Who watches your vlogs/videos?

- Who is your favourite vlogger right now and why do you like them?
- Do you use any tools to block or report people who are mean?
- If one of your friends vlogged something that made you feel uncomfortable or you thought was risky, what would you do?

2. Create a family vlog or blog

Why not sit down with your child and a family vlog (or blog). A family vlog or blog can be an excellent way of documenting through a digital scrapbook capturing family experiences, interests, achievements and memories and can be a fun and it can be a creative activity which can be done together. It also gives the opportunity of reinforcing and discussing online safety messages with your child.

Digital health warning

You can store your vlog privately without sharing it on social media. Please note that sharing family information online can raise privacy and safety concerns, and lead to attracting on wanted attention or exposure to cyber bullying or trolling. Be mindful that some children may also dislike having their lives documented. 'Sharenting', with parents oversharing their family lives (and their child's lives) online can be scrutinised ethically as personal information is over shared in a public forum.

For further information

Internet Matters – https://www.internetmatters.org/resources/parents-guide-to-live-streaming-and-vlogging/

References

Ofcom (2024) *A Window into Young Children's Online Worlds*. Ofcom.

Global Media Insight (2025) *YouTube Statistics 2025 (Demographics, Users by Country and More*. Global Media Insight, https://www.globalmediainsight.com/blog/youtube-users-statistics/

Ofcom (2023) *Teens on Screens: Life online for children and young adults revealed*. Ofcom.

Ofcom (2025) *Children and Parents: Media Use and Attitudes Report*. Ofcom.

W – Digital wellbeing

The chapter will cover:

- An overview of what digital wellbeing means.
- The benefits of digital technology on children and young people's wellbeing.
- Views of parents, carers and professionals of young people's digital use and wellbeing.
- How we can practically support the digital wellbeing of neurodivergent children and young people.
- Views of parents, carers and professionals on neurodiversity and digital mental wellbeing.
- Practical tips and activities to support children and young people's and neurodivergent children's digital mental wellbeing.

What is digital wellbeing?

Wellbeing is essential for all of us, especially children and young people, when using digital technology. Digital wellbeing is about how the online world can affect our mental health as well as our physical health. It is crucial for children and young people as their adolescent brains are still developing and excessive, inappropriate, unsafe and unbalanced use can negatively impact their mental, emotional and physical health.

The benefits of digital technology on children and young people's wellbeing

Digital technology has many benefits for enhancing our mental health and wellbeing (although it is important to ensure all digital sites, platforms and technology are regulated). Some of the benefits include:

- Provides immediate access to **information, advice and guidance** 24 hours a day on a range of wellbeing issues and in different formats (for example, toolkits, educational resources, videos, podcasts, apps or academic articles). This information, advice and guidance can provide children and young people, parents, carers and professionals with practical skills, knowledge, information and signpost to alternative services and information.
- Supports **healthy lifestyles and physical health** through, for example, apps or wearable technology (e.g. smartwatches) which track for example, nutrition, heart rate, sleep patterns and physical activity. Some apps and sites use gamification to set challenges and goals to achieving a healthy lifestyle and behaviour change. Data-driven insights through AI and machine learning can also analyse personal date to deliver tailored health and wellbeing goals and recommendations.
- Allows us to **connect** with each other to meet peers, and others who share the same interests to build online communities and support networks (see N – Networking), share experiences and gain information, advice and support. This is especially important for those young people who are more marginalised and face social exclusion. Online engagement allows them to connect with others to share experiences and identities and foster solidarity and often emotional support.
- **Digital therapy** and e-counselling can be an alternative or additional to face-to-face therapeutic interventions. This can be through evidence-based text, chat or video platforms therapy. For many children, young people and adults, online regulated counselling and therapy can provide flexible, accessible and immediate options to receiving support and interventions. It can be cheaper, more convenient, available immediately and can be accessed in different settings (e.g. at home or in school), which does not necessarily require travel. Sessions can often be scheduled flexibly outside normal office hours and, for some young people, reduces the stigma of physically attending a counsellor's office by providing discreet access in alternative locations at a time that suits them.

- Provides **wellbeing tools** which provide techniques, support and skills to improve our mental wellbeing. There is a plethora of tools available including those that provide mindfulness, meditation and mood tracking features which can be accessed.
- Can **improve access to healthcare** through, for example, diagnostic and assessment opportunities, support waiting list management and telemedicine through remote consultations which can ultimately positively affect children and young people's wellbeing.

Parents, carers and professionals' views on children and young people's digital use and wellbeing

Parents, carers and professionals shared both the opportunities and the risks that digital use has on the wellbeing of children and young people. Many noted that digital technology could positively provide information, advice and guidance to support children and young people's wellbeing. For example, a clinician noted that:

> *"It seems that many children and young people feel comfortable on digital platforms using technology to access a wide variety of things. It allows them to seek advice without having to ask another person or let someone know how they might be feeling".*

> *"There are a lot of good websites out there, lots of good information and support that can be accessed around the clock".*

But for others, there was concern about children and young people's access to misinformation and fidelity of the information and advice that they were accessing (see F – Fake news).

The access to digital technology to provide therapeutic interventions was raised by parents, carers and professionals, to be mostly a positive opportunity. One parent stated:

"Our son (aged 13) was hesitant at first and we were cynical about how beneficial online counselling would be, but we had been waiting for face-to-face counselling for over 15 months.... we were desperate for support. The online CBT was great. He (our son) found it really helpful and particularly liked the fact he could have sessions in the evening and didn't have to travel to get help. He could access counselling in his own space at a time that suited him and what is brilliant is he didn't have to wait on another long waiting list to access the counselling."

A clinician said that:

"I am offering more and more treatment online... the feedback from young people and families is positive".

Others noted that:

"It means that children can be seen outside school hours".

"Many young people prefer to access mental health support online, especially those who may find face to face interactions difficult .... We need to give young people a choice".

Practical TIPS

Practical tips to support children and young people's digital mental wellbeing

There are various practical tips for parents, carers and professionals to help support children and young people's wellbeing, for example:

- Encourage children and young people to explore appropriate and regulated **wellbeing techniques, devices, websites and apps** that can support their wellbeing and physical health.

- Talk to children and young people about the benefits of **digital hygiene** and encourage them to review the social media platforms and sites they use. Undertake a **digital declutter** by organising files, unsubscribing from unnecessary sites and social media platforms and streamline apps that are not being used. Suggest deleting those that are not being used or having a negative impact on their wellbeing, productivity and relationships.
- Encourage them to **document the amount of time spent online** – a healthy digital routine is important for your child's wellbeing.
- Encourage children and young people to use a journal to help **document** what sites, apps and platforms are being used, for how long and how they affect both their mood and emotions.

Digital wellbeing of neurodivergent children and young people

Figure 14: Digital wellbeing priorities for neurodivergent children and young people

In addition to the benefits and practical tips for digital wellbeing already outlined, an additional set of considerations should be explored for neurodivergent children and young people which are demonstrated below:

- **Sensory needs** of a neurodivergent child are key. Multi-media technologies including games and virtual reality can help manipulate sensory, motor, interpersonal and cognitive processes. Various digital tools are available or can be adapted for neurodivergent children and young people to help manage their sensory sensitivities and help them self-regulate. For example, it can be helpful to review and adjust noise levels or the brightness of any screens to avoid sensory overload. User-friendly and simply designed platforms should be encouraged to avoid overstimulating interfaces. Noise cancelling headphones can be useful for neurodivergent children and young people to cancel background distracting noises. Digital applications can provide predictable, comforting and controlled environments for neurodivergent children and young people.
- The **digital environment** should take into consideration clearly communicated boundaries for digital usage. Clearly communicated schedules and timings of screen usage is important and provides important boundaries for children and young people. Establishing a digital routine and boundaries with children and young people provides consistency and clarity. Timers which demonstrate screen usage can help provide clear and visible time boundaries.
- It is important to minimise **distractions and focus attention** by encouraging the use of apps and sites that help a neurodivergent young person stay on task and not overload them in terms of content.
- To help promote digital mental **wellbeing** it is important to encourage positive interactions and engagement through content. Discuss which digital activities create triggers and what the triggers are – what overstimulates children and young people, what makes them happy or sad?
- **Building digital literacy** helps empower children and young people to manage their own digital mental wellbeing through usage, digital hygiene and specific digital tools to safely and confidently manage their digital environment.
- **Online safety** is imperative for any child as it is important to help them navigate their digital interactions with others safely, avoid online harms, ensure moderated safe platforms are used and reiterate the importance of identifying and reporting cyberbullying.

- Encourage **alternative offline activities** to help provide a healthy balance and promote healthy lifestyles.
- A range of **communication aids and assistive** technology can support neurodivergent children and young people and their families. Explore some of the many tools, sites and platforms that are available that promote accessibility (making sure that they are both regulated and moderated). It is important to tailor any approach for neurodivergent children and young people as digital technology can provide a key opportunity to learn new skills, enhance creativity, promote independence and help encourage social interactions.
- **Social connections**, through the use of digital technology, are key for neurodivergent children and young people as they play a key role in their emotional, cognitive and social skill development. Digital technology can be a way in which to enable this – to help them feel valued and understood, enhance self-esteem and feelings of belonging and therefore the potential to improve emotional wellbeing. For many, it can provide a comfortable and non-threatening way to connect with their peers, other neurodivergent children and young people to build bonds with others along with social connections, where face to face interaction can sometimes feel intimidating.

Potential challenges

Whilst digital technology has several benefits for neurodivergent children and young people, parents should be aware of the challenges too. For some neurodiverse children, the overwhelming influx of information and digital usage can result in overstimulation, sensory overload and impact a child's ability to maintain attention. Some neurodivergent children and young people are more prone to cyberbullying and online harms. Over reliance on digital communication also has the potential to limit face to face social interactions which could impact a child's social skill development and emotional wellbeing.

Feedback from parents and professionals on neurodiversity and digital mental wellbeing

This Guide has been shaped through consultation with parents and professionals. The majority of comments from parents and professionals shared the positive impact on children and young people's mental health. One teacher said:

"Technology can provide connection and belonging for children who might struggle, particularly neurodivergent children. There are all types of technology available now to support neurodivergent children in the classroom".

A parent shared that:

"My children are autistic and ADHD and to some extent positively use tech to decompress and self-regulate. Socially, it has a large positive impact and allows them to stay connected with their friends and peers which they otherwise wouldn't meet with, if it wasn't for their screens".

Reflecting the importance of social connections, one parent of an autistic 12-year-old son said:

"It (digital technology) allows him to socialise in a way that he's comfortable with".

Another parent of neurodivergent children said:

"Socially, it has a largely positive impact and allows them to stay connected with their friends and peers".

A mother of a 16-year-old neurodivergent child said:

"I am a mother of X who was diagnosed autistic when he was 13. His screens have been an important part of his life. In fact, you could say he was addicted! He used screens to help calm himself down – he felt safe, with his headphones on, sitting in the dark playing endless games

online, day and night. It was a battle to get him off the computer and there were many meltdowns. He couldn't self-regulate his use and I struggled with all the battles and meltdowns... For us, the school helped us work with him to co-create a reward chart for both home and school which provided a bit of a routine and some boundaries".

Activities to support children and young people's wellbeing

Try these two activities with your children.

1. Happy wellbeing activity.
2. Digital wellbeing poster.

1. Happy wellbeing activity

This activity will encourage your child to identify what elements of technology positively affect their mental wellbeing and those things that have a negative effect. Make this a fun and timed activity. Once the positive and negative aspects have been identified, encourage a conversation with them to come up with strategies to turn those things that have a negative impact on their mental health into positives.

- List the top ten things that make you happy when using digital technology, and why they make you happy?
- List the top ten things that worry you or make you sad or angry when using digital technology?
- Identify a clever idea of how to make those things that make you angry or sad when using digital technology into a positive?

2. Digital wellbeing poster

Why not encourage your child to create a poster and include all the things that help promotes digital wellbeing and resilience. Here is a poster that has been designed in collaboration with young people that you can copy or use.

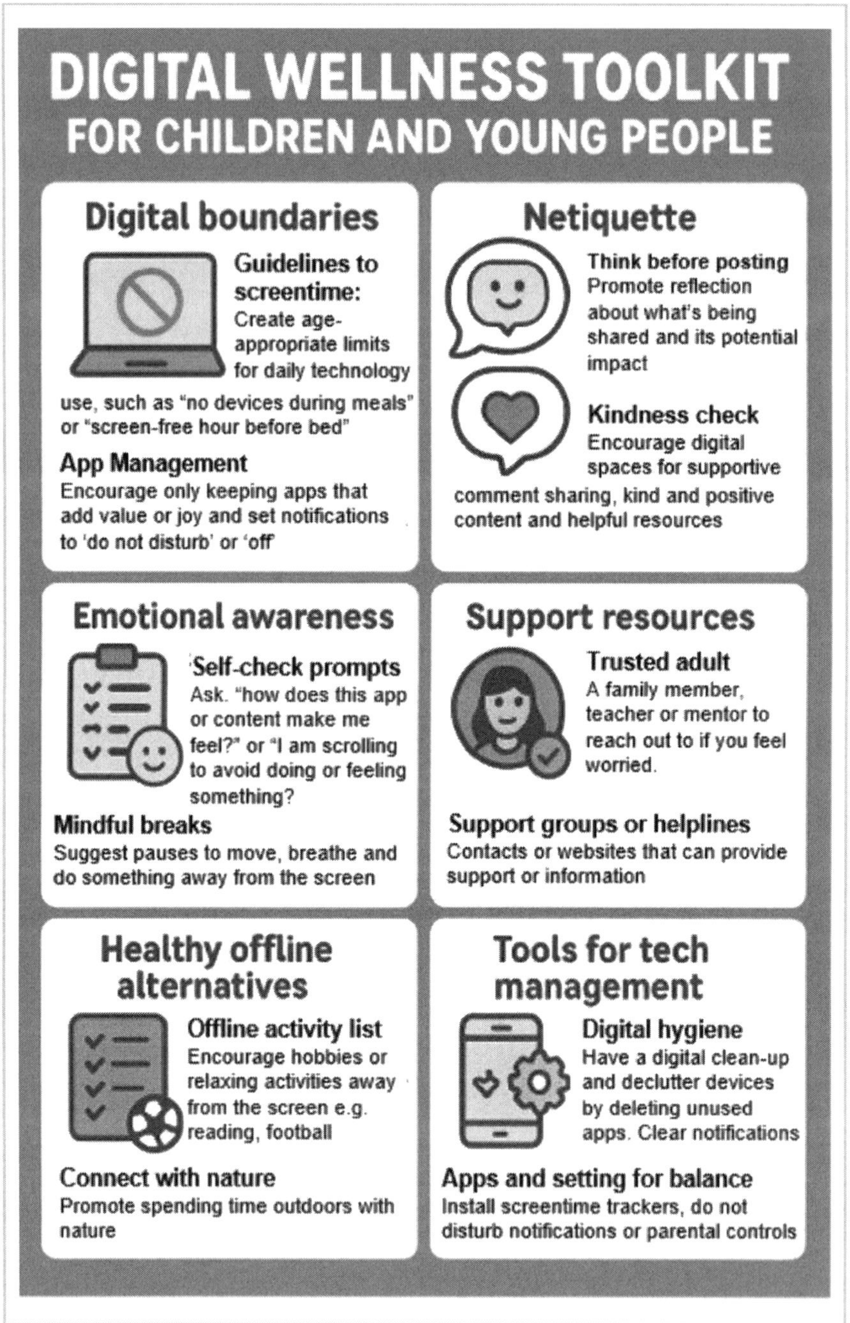
DIGITAL WELLNESS TOOLKIT
FOR CHILDREN AND YOUNG PEOPLE
Digital boundaries
Guidelines to screentime:
Create age-appropriate limits for daily technology use, such as "no devices during meals" or "screen-free hour before bed"
App Management
Encourage only keeping apps that add value or joy and set notifications to 'do not disturb' or 'off'
Netiquette
Think before posting
Promote reflection about what's being shared and its potential impact
Kindness check
Encourage digital spaces for supportive comment sharing, kind and positive content and helpful resources
Emotional awareness
Self-check prompts
Ask. "how does this app or content make me feel?" or "I am scrolling to avoid doing or feeling something?
Mindful breaks
Suggest pauses to move, breathe and do something away from the screen
Support resources
Trusted adult
A family member, teacher or mentor to reach out to if you feel worried.
Support groups or helplines
Contacts or websites that can provide support or information
Healthy offline alternatives
Offline activity list
Encourage hobbies or relaxing activities away from the screen e.g. reading, football
Connect with nature
Promote spending time outdoors with nature
Tools for tech management
Digital hygiene
Have a digital clean-up and declutter devices by deleting unused apps. Clear notifications
Apps and setting for balance
Install screentime trackers, do not disturb notifications or parental controls

For further information and support

There are a wealth of apps, platforms and sites that can support parents and children's wellbeing and whilst we do not endorse specific ones, we actively promote the importance of ensuring that you access and signpost children to regulated, monitored and evidence-based technology, platforms and sites.

Internet Matters provides a directory of wellbeing apps for children. https://www.internetmatters.org/resources/wellbeing-apps-guide-for-kids/

NSPCC, in partnership with **Ambitions about Autism**, have created a useful resource on how to support children with special educational needs when talking to people and making friends online. https://www.nspcc.org.uk/globalassets/documents/online-safety/online-safety---downloadable-resources/cso_send_talking-to-people-visual-article_jan2022.pdf

X – X-rated

The chapter will cover:

- Three X-rated online harms including online pornography, sexting and sextortion.
- An overview of the latest research.
- Views from young people, parents and professionals.
- Practical tips for parents, carers and professionals to help promote healthy sexual relationships for your child, and what to look out for if you are worried about your child and their access to indecent images or messages and sextortion.

Growing up online: distinguishing healthy development from harmful content

Children and young people naturally undergo sexual and hormonal development as part of growing up, which often leaves them vulnerable to harmful and confusing messages especially when they are exposed to pornography. Often this exposure does not reflect healthy, developmentally or age-appropriate understandings of healthy relationships, consent and intimacy. Relationships, Health and Sex Education (RHSE) in schools has a critical role in helping children distinguish between real-life emotional development and unrealistic, inappropriate and exploitative references to sex and healthy relationships.

The ubiquity of pornography

Pornography or X-rated material online is becoming more widespread as children and young people have access to indecent images at a younger and younger age. Pornography is a significant online harm which exposes children and young people to sexually explicit contents which can distort their perception of healthy relationships, consent and body image and foster misogyny and racism. Early exposure to pornographic content online, whether this is through social media or elsewhere online can lead to desensitisation and unrealistic expectations about sex. Repeated exposure can potentially lead to engaging in risky behaviours like sexting or becoming vulnerable to online grooming or sextortion.

Research on children and young people and pornography, sexting and sextortion

Parents are becoming more and more concerned about their children viewing sexual images and inappropriate content. Ofcom (2023) researched media use and attitudes of children and parents and found that:

- 75% of parents of 3–17-year-olds were concerned about their child seeing inappropriate sexual or 'adult' content online.
- 49% expressed concern about what their children were watching through TV programmes which portrayed sexual or violent contents and bad language.

Internet Matters (2024) explored the top issues of concern for parents relating to online harms. They found that:

- 44% were worried about their child receiving unwanted sexual attention from a stranger.
- 40% were concerned about their child seeing sexual content or nudity online.

Children are accessing or coming across pornography at an earlier and earlier age. Research by the Children's Commissioner (2023) suggests that:

- The average age of children seeing online pornography is 13 years old, although nearly a quarter come across online pornography by the time they are only 11 years old.

- Both girls and boys were equally as likely to see pornography by the age of 13 years old.
- 8 out of 10 young people will have come across violent pornography before they reach 18.

The UK has implemented robust legislation to tackle online harms, particularly through the Online Safety Act (2023), which empowers Ofcom to regulate digital platforms and ensure they protect users, in particular children and young people. Under this law, tech firms must take stringent measures to prevent exposure to harmful content, including online abuse, pornography, self-harm material, and misinformation. Companies must introduce age-verification systems, conduct risk assessments, and remove illegal content. Social media platforms and search engines have a legal duty to prioritise child safety and protect them against online harms, with significant penalties if they do not comply.

Online pornography, sexting and sextortion

Online pornography

There has been a global growth in internet pornography which can take the form of images and videos of people participating in sex online. As digital technology is a key part of children and young people's lives, access to pornography and the need to protect children from the harms related to online pornography is an ever-increasing global reality. Whilst some children and young people will actively seek pornography through websites or search engines, some will stumble upon it accidently on their devices, through live streaming or even advert pop-ups through social media, and some will be shown it by others.

For many young people, online pornography can be accessed due to curiosity, boredom or to find out more about sex. For many young people it is less embarrassing to learn about sex through technology than discussing it with friends and family. However, for many other children and young people, accessing online pornography can be problematic due to the dangers and risks associated to its exposure and contents. Online pornography can also portray unhealthy and unrealistic attitudes towards sexual relationships. It can also reinforce gender-biased stereotypes, unhealthy and distorted body image, promote unsafe sexual practices and, in some cases, expose and normalise violent or aggressive sexual behaviour.

Sexting

Sexting is sending, forwarding or receiving sexually explicit messages, semi-nude, nude or suggestive photos or even videos, often done via text, email, posting on social media or social networking sites.

Why do young people sext?

For some young people it is a way of feeling connected and communicating within a relationship, especially long-distance relationships. Some young people use it to flirt, experiment with fantasy or help them find intimacy and can be a way of showing affection.

Parents and professionals highlighted the use of Snapchat as a social networking site which was used by young people for sexting because messages disappeared after a short time having been received. They felt that many young people feel safe that they can send photos or images which can be automatically deleted; however, people who receive these images can save, copy them and distribute them.

Sexting can be illegal if linked to children under 18. The law states that it is an offence to make, distribute, possess or show indecent images of anyone under the age of 18 even if they are created through consent (Section 1 Protection of Children Act 1978). If a child under 18 distributes indecent images, it is likely that the Police would be involved but unlikely that it would result in prosecution.

Sextortion

Sextortion or sex extortion is a form of blackmail when people are tricked or forced to send intimate photos (often nudes or semi-nudes, sometimes known as 'dick pics') and then threatened that these will be shared publicly to friends and family unless money or further images are handed over. Sextortion perpetrators are often able to gain access to contact lists through social media accounts – this may include friends, family and work/school colleagues.

Perpetrators of sextortion can often use fake identities to blackmail young people, and some can be part of an organised criminal gang. They often target young people through gaming, social media or online dating apps. A perpetrator relies on young person paying money whilst feeling ashamed, embarrassed, humiliated and worried of intimate images being shared and too scared to report cases to the Police.

Parents, carers and professionals' views on online pornography, sexting and sextortion

Parents and professionals who were consulted as part of the development of this Guide identified concerns about online pornography, sexting and sextortion, commenting that:

"It really scares me that my daughter is in her room, on her screen…my biggest fear is that she is being exposed to sexual content, and I won't even know about it".

"The images on social media platforms seem so highly sexualised – there is a very thin line about what constitutes pornography and what does not…but it is really worrying".

"The issue is the algorithms – once they view these images, they get sent more and more of the same".

"I was shocked that my daughter was receiving and sending sexual messages with her boyfriend. She is only 14. She told me that her friends did the same…we talked about it together".

Feedback from a young person on his experience of sextortion:

"My friend (18 years old) phoned me and said he had met a girl online through a website, and the girl had persuaded him to take some 'dick pics'. The girl was a scam, and the scammers contacted him, resharing the pictures he had sent to the girl along with a screenshot of contact details of all his family, friends and workmates. The scammers made him initially pay £20 in Xbox vouchers and

then asked for a further £120 in similar vouchers. He had to take a screenshot of the voucher codes and send them to the scammers. My friend was mortified, embarrassed and so scared that he sent the vouchers. He was too scared to tell anyone especially the Police, in case the photos were shared. He now really struggles with anxiety… this has really affected his self-confidence".

Practical TIPS Practical tips for parents and professionals to help promote healthy sexual relationships

There are various tips for parents and professionals to help you promote healthy sexual relationships with your child. These tips will also help you to know what to look out for if you are worried about your child being the victim of sextortion.

Practical tips on online pornography

- Signs to look out for which could explain that your child has been viewing online pornography:
  - Inappropriate and explicit pop-ups on web browsers and deleted browsing history.
  - Changes in behaviour or the use of more sexualised language.
  - Unexplained charges and payments.
- Young people are often embarrassed to talk to adults about pornography and often parents, carers and professionals can find it daunting to start a conversation about sex with young people. However, it is really important to talk openly about online pornography and the risks associated with it.
- If your child sees something illegal, or online images or contents that worries them, report it to a trusted adult or through the Child Exploitation and Online Protection Command (CEOP).
- Avoid children accidently stumbling across pornography online by ensuring that parental controls are established on all devices.

Practical tips on sexting, preventing sextortion and how to deal with sextortion

Key red flags that you should encourage children and young people to look out for online to prevent them being the victim of sextortion can include:

- Requests to follow on social media by people that you don't know or recognise.
- Sexualised comments or questions whilst communicating.
- Being sent intimate photos or pictures which then leads to being asked to reciprocate and share your own intimate photos.
- Promises that photos will be instantly deleted.
- Making excuses that webcams or microphones do not work.

Practical tips for parents, carers and professionals to support a child or young person who is the victim of sextortion:

- Talk and keep talking to your child about the risks of sharing intimate photos or messages online. It is important to convey that they are not to blame and do not need to deal with it alone.
- If your child is involved in sextortion – contact the Police immediately. You can also report sextortion to the Child Exploitation and Online Protection (CEOP) website.
- Don't delete any messages, photos or videos that have been shared – these might be needed as evidence.
- Don't let your child engage any further conversation with the perpetrator and don't send any money.
- If your child is or has been a victim of sextortion, seek support.

For further help and information

If you have any concerns about the safety of a child or young person, you should contact the police. Additional support can be found:

CEOP (Child Exploitation and Online Protection Command) – for concerns about grooming, exploitation or sexual abuse online – www.ceop.police.uk

Internet Safety Centre – www.saferinternet.org.uk

Report Remove – Internet Watch Foundation (IWF) and Yoiti to help remove any sexual image or video from the internet - https://www.childline.org.uk/info-advice/bullying-abuse-safety/online-mobile-safety/report-remove/

SWGfl offer a free helpline to professionals working with children and young people with any online safety issue – https://swgfl.org.uk/helplines/professionals-online-safety-helpline/

ThinkUKnow provides advice on how to deal with a child sharing nude images – www.thinkuknow.co.uk

Children's Commissioner (2023) *Evidence on pornography's influence on harmful sexual behaviour among children*. Children's Commissioner.

Internet Matters/BMG (2024) *Children's Wellbeing in a Digital World: Year Three Index Report 2024*. Internet Matters in collaboration with BMG.

Ofcom (2023) *Children and Parents: Media Use and Attitudes*. Ofcom.

Online Safety Act (2023)

Y – Young people and gambling

The chapter will cover:

- The latest research on online gambling.
- Different types of gambling online.
- How to spot any signs that your child has an unhealthy relationship with gambling.
- Views of parents, carers and professionals about online gambling.
- Practical tips and activities to tackle online gambling.

The rise and accessibility of online gambling

Children and young people have increasing access and exposure to online gambling, often through gaming or advertising. But how do we know if our children are betting online and, more importantly, how do we notice the signs of an unhealthy relationship with gambling? Whilst most young people will have no issues with gambling, for some, gambling can be a risky activity which can get out of control and affect their mental health. For many children and young people, online gambling and gaming (see G – Gaming) are becoming increasingly intertwined through, for example, the use of in-game purchasing and loot boxes and sports betting through apps.

Online gambling refers to using online platforms or digital devices to 'make a stake or risk money or anything of value on the outcome of something involving chance' (Big Deal). Although most gambling is illegal for anyone under 18, children and young people may still engage in different types of gambling for several reasons either because they find it fun, out of boredom or for the chance of taking a risk and winning money or something of value.

Over the last few years there has been a significant growth in online gambling which affects both adults and children. The UK online gambling market is valued at £6.9 billion and is projected to grow to £12.68 billion by 2033 (Gambling Commission 2024). The gambling industry is a popular and lucrative business and gambling is more accessible than ever before, especially online.

Research and online gambling

The Gambling Commission (2024a; 2024b) found that:

- 8% of young people had reported having had some experience of online gambling which included casino games, bingo and National Lottery online.
- Young people (8%) are actively engaging in online gambling, often using their parents' accounts or betting through gaming (e.g. with in-game items like loot boxes) and the majority were doing so with their parent's permission.
- The majority (68%) of young people were aware that they could buy in-game items (e.g. loot boxes).
- A smaller percentage (37%) were aware that they could bet with these in-game items.
- Over half of young people had paid for in-game items and 'mods'.
- A third had paid for loot boxes.
- 4% had bet with in-game items.

Most young people used gift cards, virtual money and money from their own bank to pay for in-game items and 'mods', whereas virtual currency was the most common way for young people (58%) to pay to open loot boxes (Gambling Commission, 2024a).

Different types of gambling

Whilst most gambling is illegal for anyone under the age of 18, there are different types of online gambling which involve either games of chance or skill using money through a variety of devices including either a laptop, computer or mobile device. Do you recognise any of the examples of online gambling listed below?

- **eSports betting** involves predicting sports results and placing a bet on an outcome. Some e-sports betting sites even encourage inter-play gambling for individuals to place bets whilst a live sports event is happening.
- **Sweepstake casinos** are often facilitated through dual currency systems (for example, gold coins, dice or credits) which do not necessarily have real world value but earned through each game. Examples of sweepstake casino games can include for example, virtual roulette, poker, blackjack and online slot machines.
- **In-game items:**
  - **Skin gambling** – skins are cosmetic items that players can use to adapt the appearance of their character, avatar or weapons during an online game. If a specific skin is scarce, they become collectable items and are often awarded through a game, purchased with real money or in-game cash. Skins can also be traded on, bet on or sold for real cash on third party websites.
  - **Loot boxes** contain items that will help you advance in an online game; like skins, players pay to open without knowing what is inside. A loot box may contain items which will be valuable to a game but there is also a risk that they may not and therefore be worthless. Loot boxes are not classified as gambling although there is research which identifies concerns that they may lead to harmful gambling. Gaming influencers on social media who livestream the opening of loot boxes are also popular with young people.

Whilst skin gambling and loot boxes are very popular amongst children and young people, it is often perceived to be a form of gaming rather than gambling. In the UK, loot boxes are not formally classed as gambling, however the Gambling Commission confirms that gaming can be a route into betting which suggests that many children are gambling without even realising it.

What are some of the signs that a child has an unhealthy relationship with gambling?

Some of the behaviours that your child may display that could be linked with online gambling could include:

- Mood changes and/or low mood and becoming easily agitated.
- Being withdrawn or unusually quiet.
- Gambling websites appearing on their browser history.
- Being defensive and evasive about their online activity if asked.
- Being secretive about money and getting cross if asked about how money is spent.
- Money being borrowed on a regular basis or taking from friends or family.
- Spending more time alone and avoiding social situations.

Parents, carers and professionals' views on online gambling

Parents in particularly identified their concerns with online gambling. One parent of an 18-year-old son said:

> *"When we realised our son was gambling online after constantly asking to borrow money, we helped him put blocking software on his computer but what doesn't help is so many betting ads popping up online".*

Another parent said that:

> *"I never thought (my son) would steal from us! I think he is addicted to some of these sites. What is worse, he plays some of them with his mates but most of the time it is with people he doesn't know from all over the world. Goodness knows who they are".*

Another parent said:

> *"I know how addictive it is myself, I started playing online slots on my phone. I did it when I was bored and then realised, I was spending hours playing. I wasted so much money and then I became depressed. It is easy for kids to access these games".*

Practical TIPS Practical tips to support children and young people on online gambling

There are various practical things that parents and professionals can do to help support your child understand the risks and consequences of online gambling. For example:

- Talk about gambling with children and young people regularly is important. Be **open and honest and create a space to allow your child** to talk with you about the risks and consequences of online gambling. It is important to let your child know that they are not being judged by creating a safe place for any conversation. Pick your moment to start a discussion about the impact of gambling, perhaps by choosing a time when a gambling advertisement is on TV or after they have finished playing an online game. Ask them about any potential peer pressure amongst their friends and in social situations.
- Try and **lead by example** by addressing your own gambling and gaming habits.
- Try and encourage children and young people to develop **healthy saving and budgeting habits**. Promote the value of money by helping them understand how to manage their money, how to budget and save, to help them steer away from spending their money on any gambling activity. Discuss the financial consequences of gambling, explain how gambling odds work and reiterate the benefits of saving and growing their money over time.

- Schools should be teaching children about online gambling unhealthy behaviours as part of the Relationship Health and Sexual Education curriculum. Why not **approach your school** to find out more about what is being taught and if there is any information the school can provide for parents.
- **Use blocking software** for betting and gambling websites or features. There are two kinds of blocking software – gambling-specific which blocks gambling websites and general blocking software which blocks any sites and sets access permission and parental controls.

Activity – conversation starter

Be curious and open in your discussions to encourage healthy digital online activity. Create a regular and calm space for discussion at times when you will have their full attention (e.g. after they have played a game, in the car or during mealtimes) rather than after a disagreement about time spent on screens. Examples of conversation starters include:

- What is your favourite game? Does it have loot boxes or chests? How do they work?
- Have you bought any in-game extras when you are playing a game online? How did this make you feel?
- Why do you think games use loot boxes or in-game purchases? How do gaming companies make money by promoting loot boxes or in-game purchases?
- Are you aware of people spending too much money on online games or gambling? Why do you think they do this? What could this money be spent on instead?
- What are you saving up for at the moment? What are you hoping to buy?

For further information and support on online gambling

There are a number of organisations that offer support on gambling including online gambling for young people, their parents, carers and professionals:

Internet Matters Online gaming advice hub
https://www.internetmatters.org/advice/by-activity/online-gaming-advice-hub/

Big Deal – Resources, advice and support for parents and professionals and a Young People's Service. www.bigdeal.org.uk

GamCare's Young People's Support Service – free confidential support for under 18 year olds affected by gambling. https://www.gamcare.org.uk/get-support/young-peoples-support-service/

Ygam (Young Gamers and Gamblers Education Trust) – provides resources and support for young people struggling with gaming and gambling. www.ygam.org

The National Centre for Gaming Disorders (cnwl.nhs.uk) is a multi-disciplinary clinic in the UK that provides treatment for people in England, aged 13 years and over, who have difficulty controlling their video game use and the impact it has on their lives. They also offer parents, guardians and family members support alongside the person gaming.

References

Gambling Commission (2024a) *Young People and Gambling 2024: Official Statistics*. Gambling Commission.

Gambling Commission (2024b) *Industry Statistics – November 2024*. Gambling Statistics and Research Release. Gambling Commission.

https://www.sphericalinsights.com/reports/united-kingdom-online-gambling-market

Z – Zoning Out

The chapter will cover:

- What is meant by the term 'zoning out'.
- Why children and young people scroll endlessly.
- Spotting the signs of mindless scrolling and zoning out.
- Views of parents, carers and professionals.
- Practical tips and activities to help encourage children to overcome mindless scrolling and zoning out.

What is 'zoning out'?

Have you noticed yourself or your child getting lost in their phones, completely absorbed and disconnected from the world around you? Zoning out online is a common way in which children and young people use technology to disassociate themselves from everyday life. For many this can be a result of being stressed, bored, anxious or even a way to cope with the real world. Zoning out can be a way of escaping society and switching off from reality, which for many children and young people releases stress, or stops them feeling overwhelmed, sad or anxious.

What does the research say about children and young people's online use?

On a daily basis we are all spending more and more time online. Ofcom (2024) found that:

- Adults spend the equivalent of 56 days a year online.
- Children and young people spend on average 3 hours and 5 minutes accessing the internet through smartphones, computers and tablets every day.
- 18- to 24-year-olds spend approximately 4 hours 36 minutes each day online.

For children and young people this can include a considerable amount of time mindless scrolling.

Why do children and young people engage in mindless scrolling?

For many children and young people mindless scrolling is a way of zoning out. Mindless scrolling, also known as zombie or infinite scrolling, refers to spending extended time on social media with no specific purpose. With access to so many devices and constant access to a smartphone, many fall into the habit of mindlessly scrolling and often not even realising they are doing it or for how long they have been scrolling.

Doomscrolling or 'doom surfing' is also infinite scrolling but specifically refers to the habit of scrolling for bad news and negative contents. Prolonged exposure to negative information can have an impact on mental wellbeing by increasing stress and anxiety levels. Distressing images can reinforce feelings of doom and helplessness, increase anxiety and low mood.

There are many reasons why mindless scrolling is so addictive, for some it is for entertainment and escapism; for others it is to alleviate boredom or to kill time. Scrolling releases dopamine which is a 'feel-good' chemical high which is linked to pleasure and reward. For many children and young people, the fear of missing out (FOMO) on news and updates, keeps them scrolling on their phones for hours.

Social media sites rely on this and actively encourage infinite scrolling by using never ending bite sized streams of posts. The algorithms on social media are set so that we receive contents that we are interested in or enjoy, hence keeping us scrolling longer.

What are the possible signs for mindless scrolling?

There are many signs that could indicate that a child or young person is mindlessly scrolling. For example:

- Inability to control how much time is spent online.
- Lying to others about how much time is spent online.
- Endless scrolling even when undertaking everyday tasks eg going to the toilet, washing up, watching TV.
- Feeling irritable and anxious when devices or internet access is taken away from them.

Parents, carers and professionals' views on zoning out and mindless scrolling

Many parents and professionals noted their concerns about children and young people's excessive online use. For example, a teacher stated that:

> *"The amount of time spent on all these platforms is alarming and I can definitely see the links between this and the impact on my pupils' mental health."*

Several parents noted the amount of time their children spent:

> *"scrolling on their screens but not really retaining anything they were looking at";*
>
> *"scrolling whilst they are actively doing other things like watching tv or having a conversation with their friends."*

When asked, a 16-year-old boy shared that he was aware of zoning out through endless scrolling but he had adopted coping mechanisms to help him manage his online use. He said:

> *"I scroll all the time …. on TikTok mostly and also Instagram… fashion, lifestyle, and cooking reels. I usually scroll for hours after college and in the evenings. It helps me relax, zone out and*

decompress… I don't have to think about anything. To help me from scrolling, I have set my own screen-time break reminders for every half an hour and one at 11pm as a sleep check. They are really good as they help me check I am not scrolling for too long".

Practical TIPS — Practical tips to help encourage children to overcome mindless scrolling and zoning out

- **Keep track and manage your screentime**, in particular time you and your child spend scrolling mindlessly. For example, turn off notifications, and download apps that can monitor and track screentime use.
- **Set screentime limits** – why not set screentime targets for the day and week and see how you can reduce screentime?
- **Set screen time breaks** – lots of social media platforms allow you to set reminders of how long you have been using them; setting an alarm to remind your child to take a break can also be useful to prevent them from 'losing' time scrolling.
- **Recognise and remove triggers and create positive distractions.** For example, if your child reaches for their phone as soon as they wake up, find a distraction to create different habits or leave phones downstairs.
- **Encourage a healthy balance between online and offline activities** – seek other hobbies or activities that do not rely on digital technology.
- **Discuss online habits** with your child to find out what sites they visit and apps they use and for how long and why. Why not have a digital spring clean by reviewing what apps, social media accounts are being used and deleting those that aren't used.
- **Turn off or silence notifications** on computers and phones so that the constant 'ping' of a notification does not draw you or your child to your devices to respond immediately.
- Be a **healthy digital role model** by not mindlessly scrolling yourself. Children will learn by watching what their parents or other adults do! They also notice if parents choose them over a device.

Activities to prevent children from mindlessly scrolling

Two activities have been developed for you to complete with children and young people to prevent them mindlessly scrolling and zoning out:

1. How to stop yourself from scrolling checklist.
2. Screentime tracker.

1. How to stop yourself from scrolling checklist

To avoid mindless scrolling, here are some alternative fun things to do:

- Draw or paint a picture
- Write a journal
- Go for a cycle
- Do a workout
- Write a letter to a friend
- Meet your friends
- Tidy your room
- Enjoy a relaxing bath
- Play a board game

- Go for a walk

- Do a puzzle

- Bake a cake

Why not make your own 'Stop Yourself from Scrolling' checklist ?

2. Screen time tracker

Tracking your own and supporting your child's screen time is a useful activity. This activity not only identifies how much time is spent using different devices but also help set goals for the following week. Whilst there are a number of digital apps that can help monitor screen time, this version has been created for you to print out and complete – why not display a copy on the kitchen fridge or in a bedroom?

Screen Time Tracker

	Phone	Computer	Video Games	Tablet	TV	Other	Daily Minutes
Monday							
Tuesday							
Wednesday							
Thursday							
Friday							
Saturday							
Sunday							
						Total weekly minutes	
						Screentime goal for next week	

References

Ofcom (2024) *Online Nation*. Ofcom.

Section 3: Moving forward

Conclusions

This *A to Z Guide on Children's Digital Mental Health* is a practical and accessible tool created for parents, carers and professionals who support children and young people in today's increasingly digital world. With technology playing a central role in children's lives, understanding its impact on children's mental health is more important than ever before. Each letter of the alphabet introduces a key issue which was raised as a priority through consultation with parents and professionals. It covers a wealth of topics from Artificial Intelligence through to body image and appearance, gaming, influencers, misogyny, online safety, and zoning out from excessive use. It provides clear insights, current research, signs to look out for, conversations starters, some of the key challenges and practical tools and activities to help parents and professionals support their children's digital mental wellbeing.

Designed to empower parents and professionals with the knowledge and confidence to support children and young people's digital mental wellbeing, this Guide blends up-to-date research with real-world strategies and practical tools with activities. It encourages healthy open conversations, promotes digital literacy, and emphasizes the importance of balance, boundaries, and empathy in managing screen use. Whether you're a parent navigating daily challenges at home or a professional working with children and young people, this Guide offers a valuable foundation for understanding and addressing the digital factors and challenges that influence children's digital mental health.

Whatever type of digital parent or digital professional you are, it's important to remember that you don't need to have all the answers – you just need to be present, informed, and open to communicating and learning alongside your child. The digital world can feel overwhelming and exhausting, but with the right tools and a compassionate approach, the priority is helping to guide your child toward healthy, balanced digital use. Your efforts to understand your child's online experiences, set boundaries, and maintain open communication can help make a meaningful difference. By staying engaged and supportive, you can help to build your child's digital resilience, confidence and mental wellbeing in a world where digital life is part of everyday life.

The last words of the A to Z Guide belong to one of the parents who shared their views about children's digital mental wellbeing:

> *"We do need to be aware of some of the challenges that our children face in this online world that they are growing up in, especially on keeping them safe and happy, so that they can live their best digital lives... There is so much pressure on them from being online to live a perfect life! There are definitely aspects of digital tech that can be a real, positive thing for children to help their mental wellbeing, their learning and keep them connected with their friends".*

For further information and resources

Empowering Digital Lives – www.empoweringdigitallives.com

Glossary

This Glossary includes a list of digital terms used in this Guide and their explanations. How many of these terms are you aware of?

Algorithms are tools used by technology companies to watch our behaviour to determine what we are accessing online. As a result, they can channel specific content based on our online 'interests'.

AI (Artificial Intelligence) – intelligent machines which think and learn like humans. AI systems can process information, make decisions, and adapt to new situations to perform tasks that would typically require human intelligence.

Augmented reality (AR) – brings together the physical and virtual world by superimposing animations or computer-generated images.

Avatar – digital representation of yourself which is used online..

Bitcoin – virtual currency (cryptocurrency) which acts as money or a form of payment outside the control of government or banks.

Blogging – sharing written thoughts, ideas and experiences online.

Body checking – compulsive behaviour of scrutinising your body shape, size and weight in comparison to other bodies portrayed online.

Catfishing – when people create a false identity to lure a young person into a relationship.

Clickbait – sensationalised or misleading content that tricks to tempt people into clicking onto a link.

Cyberbullying – bullying that takes place online (e.g. through social networks, gaming or phone).

Cyberflashing – sending explicit images or messages to someone without their consent.

Dark web – can only be accessed through specific software and allows those who use it to communicate anonymously. It can be used to hide people's identity, share inappropriate contents and carry out illegal and criminal activity.

Deep fake is a fake image, video or audio which is created using AI to imitate another person.

Deep web is part of the World Wide Web that is hidden from the public, often behind security 'walls' protected by passwords (eg online banking, institutional intranets or databases).

Digital footprint – online history of activity including social media activity, email communications and website access records. Digital footprint is often permanent.

Digital self-harm – when someone posts hurtful and negative comments about themselves on online.

Dissing – spreading unkind information about someone else online through private messages or public posts.

Doomscrolling – compulsive desire to continuously scroll through bad news or negative contents online.

Doxing – posting or sharing personal information about someone without their consent, often for malicious reasons.

Esports betting – predicting sports results and placing a bet on an outcome online.

Fake news – news that is not true because it is either completely made up or the facts within the news story have been changed. Fake news through social media can include news stories, adverts or photo images.

Flaming – posting insulting content online to provoke a reaction or upset someone.

Fear of missing out (FOMO) – Fear of missing out from online conversations, information or messages.

Generative Artificial Intelligence – form of AI than produces text, images or audio following a prompt.

Geotracking – is using technology to identify a person's location.

Griefing – harassing or sabotaging others online especially during online gaming.

Hate speech or online hate – communication that is abusive or discriminates against a person linked to their gender identity, race, religion and beliefs, sexual orientation or disability.

Incel – online subculture of people who believe that they are involuntarily celibate, often males who are unable to find romantic partners, despite wanting to.

Influencers – people who have established credibility in a specific industry who have large audiences following them online through gaming or social media.

Kidfluencer – children under the age of sixteen who have an online presence who create content to generate views and followings.

Likes – a form of showing you like contents on social media by clicking a button.

Loot boxes – boxes that contain items that will help you advance in an online game.

Joy of missing out (JOMO) – refers to the positive feelings from intentionally disconnecting from the digital world and being 'present' in the moment.

Manosphere – spaces such as blogs, forums and websites which promote masculinity and misogyny.

Meme – image or videoclip (often humorous) which is copied and spread online.

Mindless scrolling – spending extended time on social media with no specific purpose (also known as infinite or zombie scrolling).

Misinformation – false or inaccurate information that is spread online.

Misogyny – the fundamental dislike, prejudice against or hatred of women and girls and can occur both in person and online.

Netiquette – respectful behaviour when communicating with others online.

Nomophobia – fear or anxiety of not having mobile phone connectivity.

Online hate – involves posting or sharing hateful contents including abusive or threatening language about people online, which can encourage discrimination, violence or hatred based on an individual's gender identity, race, religion and beliefs, sexual orientation or disability.

Outing – is publicly revealing personal information online without their permission and consent which often causes harm or upset.

Phishing – when individuals or groups impersonate legitimate organisations or individuals to encourage others to download attachments, share personal or financial information and data. This is often done by phone (vishing), email (email phishing), by websites or by text/SMS (smishing).

Phubbing – ignoring someone when in a social situation by paying attention to your phone instead.

Pile-ons – coordinated individuals target a specific woman or girls with often misogynistic or harassing content; image-based sexual abuse.

Roasting – making fun of someone online in a group or through social media forums (this is supposed to be light-hearted fun!)

Selfie – a digital photograph or video of yourself taken by yourself.

Selfie-harm – a digital photograph or video that is taken of yourself and digitally edited and distorted which is a result or causes feelings of anxiety.

Sexting – sending, forwarding or receiving sexually explicit messages, semi-nude, nude or suggestive photos or even videos. This is often done via text, email, posting on social media or social networking sites.

Sextortion – a form of blackmail in which people are tricked or forced to send intimate photos and then threatened that these will be shared publicly to friends and family unless money is handed over.

Sharenting – parents sharing (often over sharing) content of their child online.

Skin gambling – cosmetic items that gamers can use to adapt the appearance of their character, avatar or weapons during an online game.

Smishing – using SMS or text to scam and trick others to gain personal or sensitive information.

Spear phishing – scammers targeting a specific individual or group, often through personalised communication to trick others so that they can gain personal and sensitive information.

Sockpuppet – person who posts under false and made-up profile, often to ensure anonymity and used as deception to bully or argue with others.

Social media – apps, websites, social games that connect people through creation, sharing and bringing together content amongst virtual communities and networks.

Technoference – the everyday interruptions in interpersonal interactions affecting face to face interactions, caused by the preoccupation in digital devices.

Trolling – when someone (usually anonymous) posts or comments online to deliberately provoke a reaction or argument.

Vamping – staying up late at night due to mindless scrolling, watching videos or texting.

Vishing – phone calls to scam and trick others to gain personal or sensitive information.

Vlogging – sharing pre-recorded video content online through video sharing platforms (eg Tik Tok or YouTube).

Further Information, Advice and Support

If you or any child you know is affected by issues discussed in this guide, the following organisations offer information and advice, contact:

Childline which is a free confidential service 24/7 for under 19's living in the UK www.childline.org.uk or call 0800 1111

Stop it Now is a helpline for anyone worried about child sexual abuse www.stopitnow.org.uk

Report Remove helps children under 18 in the UK to confidentially report sexual images and videos of themselves and remove them from the internet

Samaritans offers emotional support to those in distress or crisis – www.samaritans.org

Helpful organisations for parents, carers and professionals

The Safer Internet Centre – has information to help you keep your child safe. https://saferinternet.org.uk/

The **National Society for the Prevention of Cruelty to Children (NSPCC)** has an online safety hub with advice to parents and children. https://www.nspcc.org.uk/keeping-children-safe/online-safety/talking-child-online-safety/

Internet Matters provides information and advice to parents and carers to help their child navigate the digital world. https://www.internetmatters.org/

Childnet provides educational resources and advice to help children, parents and schools navigate online risks. https://www.childnet.com/

Parentzone provides information and resources for parents. https://parentzone.org.uk/

Empowering Digital Lives – www.empoweringdigitallives.com